CAMBRIDGE MUSIC HANDBOOKS

Brahms: Clarinet Quintet

CAMBRIDGE MUSIC HANDBOOKS

GENERAL EDITOR Julian Rushton

Brahms: Clarinet Quintet

Colin Lawson

CAMBRIDGE
UNIVERSITY PRESS

CAMBRIDGE UNIVERSITY PRESS
Cambridge, New York, Melbourne, Madrid, Cape Town, Singapore, São Paulo

Cambridge University Press
The Edinburgh Building, Cambridge CB2 2RU, UK

Published in the United States of America by Cambridge University Press, New York

www.cambridge.org
Information on this title: www.cambridge.org/9780521581936

First published 1998

A catalogue record for this publication is available from the British Library

Library of Congress Cataloguing in Publication data

Lawson, Colin (Colin James)
Brahms, Clarinet quintet / Colin Lawson.
p. cm. – (Cambridge music handbooks)
Includes bibliographical references and index.
ISBN 0 521 58193 1 (hardback). – ISBN 0 521 58831 6 (paperback).
1. Brahms, Johannes, 1833–1897. Quintets, clarinet, violins, viola, violoncello,
op. 115, B minor.
I. Title. II. Series.
ML410.B8L3 1998
785'.44195'092–dc21 97–5990 CIP MN

ISBN-13 978-0-521-58193-6 hardback
ISBN-10 0-521-58193-1 hardback

ISBN-13 978-0-521-58831-7 paperback
ISBN-10 0-521-58831-6 paperback

Transferred to digital printing 2005

Contents

Contents

Illustrations

Preface

Brahms's Clarinet Quintet was immediately recognised as a wonderful achievement on its appearance in 1891 and it has retained the ability to claim the hearts and minds of players and audiences ever since. Nowadays there is likely to be little dissent from the forthright assertion in the fifth edition of *Grove's Dictionary of Music and Musicians* that 'for emotional intensity and beauty of tone-colour the Clarinet Quintet may well claim the top-most place in Brahms's chamber music'.[1] Indeed, this observation forms part of an adulatory tradition dating back to the years immediately following Brahms's death in 1897. As early as 1905 his biographer Florence May described it as a beautiful and now favourite work, containing the 'richest fruits of the golden harvest of the poet's activity'.[2] Her evocative style of writing nicely encapsulates the spirit of the Quintet, though in terms characteristic of the earlier rather than the latter part of the twentieth century:

> Here 'the brooks of life are flowing as at high noon', though the tone of gentle loving regret which pervades the four movements, and holds the heart of the listener in firm grip, suggests the composer's feeling that the evening is not far away from him in which no man may work. A fulness of rich melody, a luscious charm of tone, original effects arising from the treatment of the clarinet, 'olympian' ease and mastery, distinguish every movement of this noble and attractive work, which, taking its hearers by storm on its first production, has grown more firmly rooted to the hearts of musicians and laymen with each fresh hearing. In the middle section of the second movement Brahms has written for the clarinet a number of quasi-improvisatory passages embracing the entire extent of the compass, which are supported by the strings, and which, when competently performed, are of surprisingly attractive effect.

Brahms's innovative absorption of the Hungarian folk tradition in the Adagio of the Quintet has remained a special focus of attention.

But overall, succeeding generations have found it difficult effectively to articulate the way in which Brahms works his special magic. As Walter Frisch has recently observed, musical analysis and criticism too often fall short of communicating either a conscious intellectual admiration for Brahms's technical achievement or a less voluntary enchantment at the aesthetic experience.[3] Frisch's own book fruitfully continues Schoenberg's discussion of Brahms's procedures of thematic continuity and economy – for which Schoenberg coined the term 'developing variation' – in an attempt to unveil the most compelling qualities of Brahms's music. The analytical and contextual chapters in this book will indeed attempt to discover the source of its undeniable 'magic'.

While representing a culmination of Brahms's achievement as a composer of chamber music, the Quintet also occupies a special place in the history of the clarinet. By the time it was composed, there had already been a number of remarkable collaborations between clarinettists and composers.[4] Mozart's Clarinet Concerto bears witness to his friendship with Anton Stadler and dates from exactly a hundred years before Brahms's masterpiece. At the beginning of the nineteenth century there were fruitful partnerships between Weber and Heinrich Baermann and between Spohr and Simon Hermstedt during a period in which Weber produced a highly successful (if essentially *concertante*) Clarinet Quintet. Brahms's encounter with the Meiningen clarinettist Richard Mühlfeld towards the end of his life is especially remarkable because at the time he had already announced his retirement from composition. Furthermore, despite the clarinet's prominence within the Romantic orchestra, its position in chamber music had been in a state of sorry decline for a considerable period when Brahms embarked upon his Clarinet Trio and Quintet of 1891 and the two Sonatas of 1894. Notwithstanding some fine sets of character pieces with piano (notably by Schumann), there was scarcely any chamber music of the period in which the clarinet was truly integrated within an ensemble. In this respect Brahms produced a worthy successor to Mozart's Quintet K581, at the same time influencing later composers to an enormous degree. Brahms's resulting challenge to the performer was nicely characterised by Reginald Kell, one of the work's foremost interpreters: 'Clarinetists who are not fully developed musically and are happy just playing the instrument instead of using it to music's end would be well advised to turn their attention to a less complex style'.[5]

The special attraction of the clarinet for Brahms was captured with singular objectivity by the American writer Daniel Gregory Mason:

> The clarinet ... is no less romantic in expression and luscious in tone-color than the horn, while far more various in tone and flexible in articulation. It rivals indeed the violin in the variety of its tone-color in different registers (if not quite in intimate human feeling in its expression), and equals the piano in flexibility, adding a certain indescribable sort of voluble neatness peculiar to itself. It has three separate registers, each strongly characterized and each appealing potently to the musical nature of the mature Brahms. Its upper register is a clear and lyric soprano, slightly less sensitive than that of the violin but of an incomparable roundness and clarity. The middle register has a sort of mysterious hollowness, a sighing softness that Brahms uses *con amore*. Above all, the lower register, the so-called 'chalumeau', is dark, sober, even menacing at times, in a degree equalled by no other instrument ... Finally the extraordinary flexibility and smoothness of utterance peculiar to this instrument make available not only such impassioned gipsy-like recitatives as those of the *Adagio* of the Quintet, but the neat dovetailing of intricate figuration between piano and clarinet so fascinating in the finale of the E flat sonata. No wonder the clarinet opened to Brahms what is virtually a new vein in his genius.[6]

In examining Brahms's relationship with the clarinet, this Handbook investigates Brahms's orchestral treatment of the instrument prior to the collaboration with Mühlfeld, as well as the implications of the Quintet (and to a lesser degree the Trio and Sonatas) for later composers. Chapter 6 reflects some of my own current preoccupations relating to Brahms performance practice, and was written during a period when I was fortunate enough to take delivery of a pair of specially commissioned copies of the Baermann-Ottensteiner clarinets used by Mühlfeld.[7]

It is a pleasure to thank a large number of friends and relatives for their help, advice and inspiration in the preparation of this book. My love of the Brahms Clarinet Quintet developed many years ago, when my formative years as a clarinettist benefited from unstinting parental support and from Thea King's inspired tuition. Later immersion in period performance brought me into contact with Nicholas Shackleton, who has always been generous enough to place at my disposal his unrivalled knowledge of surviving instruments world-wide. The Cambridge maker Daniel Bangham alerted me to the expressive potential of boxwood clarinets by producing for me many fine copies from different eras of the instrument's history. In the immediate preparation of this Handbook I have been especially grateful for a period of study leave from the University of Sheffield. My research assistant Ingrid Pearson was largely responsible for compiling Chapter 2 and for innumerable other important details in the text. Further generous bibliographical advice has come from Michael Bryant, Georgina Dobrée and Jo Rees-Davies. Pamela Weston very kindly supplied previously unpublished photographs from her own unique library. My wife Hilary has been most perceptive of all in her encouragement of the project, despite the fact that its progress has coincided with intensive periods of preparation for concerts and recordings. Lastly, Penny Souster at Cambridge University Press has created a characteristic sense of urgency, whilst offering consistent and positive support.

In the following chapters, pitch registers are indicated in the following manner: middle C just below the treble staff is indicated as c', with each successive octave higher shown as c'', c''', c'''' etc. and the octave below as c. Excerpts from Brahms's clarinet part are notated in A, sounding a minor third lower.

The nineteenth-century clarinet and its music

An integrated model: Mozart's Clarinet Quintet

There are some striking parallels between the clarinet quintets of
Mozart and Brahms, unquestionably the two greatest works for the
medium. For example, Mozart directly anticipates Brahms in his expression of underlying melancholy, whilst integrating the clarinet with
the string texture to a remarkable degree. Any survey of the nineteenth-century clarinet and its music must necessarily take as its starting point the remarkable collaboration between Mozart and Stadler,
which inspired a host of other smaller pieces besides the Clarinet
Quintet and the Concerto. Mozart's Quintet for piano and winds and
his Clarinet Trio also feature the instrument within new genres in
textures far removed from the *concertante* style which dominated wind
writing of the period. The relationship of Mozart and Stadler parallels
to an uncanny degree the meeting of Brahms and Richard Mühlfeld in
1891; a further link is that it was Mühlfeld's performance of Mozart's
Quintet which played a major part in inspiring Brahms to begin work
on his own Clarinet Quintet.

Mozart's works are of the utmost importance in the history of the
clarinet's development; they represent the culmination of a century in
which the instrument developed from its origins *c.* 1700 into a fully-
fledged solo voice.[1] By Mozart's day, the cantabile possibilities of the
instrument were increasingly recognised, the B♭ instrument rather
than the clarinet in A or C having become established as the favourite
solo instrument in concertos of the Mannheim school by Johann and
Carl Stamitz, Dimler, Eichner and others. The chalumeau register
beloved of both Mozart and Brahms was beginning to play a significant part in solo idioms, whilst leaps became part of the vocabulary as
the clarinet's potential for agility was gradually appreciated. Clarinet

writing in concertos and chamber music belies the caution with which it was handled orchestrally as late as Beethoven's first two symphonies. In its five-keyed configuration, which by this time had become the norm, the clarinet was fluent over a large compass, though only within a limited range of amenable keys. As its lyrical qualities began to be widely cultivated, Daniel Schubart's book on aesthetics characterised the Viennese clarinet as overflowing with love, with an indescribable sweetness of expression.[2]

In creating the medium of the clarinet quintet, Mozart progressed significantly beyond the *concertante* idiom which had characterised the Oboe Quartet K370 and the Flute Quartets K285, 285a, 285b and 298. In these works the wind instrument assumes the role of undisputed soloist, as in the quartets for clarinet and string trio by Carl Stamitz, of which the first set of six Op. 8 was published in Paris as early as 1773. In contrast, Mozart treats the clarinet in his Clarinet Quintet as *primus inter pares*, whilst introducing virtuoso elements effectively encompassing the range of idioms cultivated by Stadler. But in chamber music for clarinet and strings from the period between Mozart and Brahms the prevailing passion for virtuosity was always liable to tilt the instrumental balance in favour of the solo wind instrument.

Although commentators have tended to focus upon Stadler's special basset clarinet (whose range extended downwards by four extra semitones), Mozart's establishment of the A clarinet as a solo instrument has attracted somewhat less attention, and this was an achievement highly relevant to a study of Brahms's Clarinet Quintet.[3] Francoeur's *Diapason général* (Paris, 1772) had already identified the tone-qualities of each of the nine clarinets he listed: the largest G clarinet was the sweetest, saddest and most lugubrious, whilst the highest E and F clarinets were suitable only for storms and battle. Among the common middle sizes Francoeur clearly distinguished clarinets in A and Bb. The A had a very sweet sound, much less sombre than the G and with a greater range; it was suitable for tender, graceful melodies. On the other hand, the Bb had a stronger sound, which could project and was therefore suitable for the grand gestures found in symphonies and overtures. The tone-quality of A and Bb clarinets was characterised in this way by many other writers during and after Mozart's lifetime; the A was always reckoned more gentle and melancholy, sometimes even rather dull in tone. This is a feature of the clarinet which Mühlfeld must have indicated to Brahms. On the other hand, in the perception of key characteristics which were hotly debated throughout the eighteenth century and beyond, A major was usually regarded as brilliant, as for example in the second volume of Grétry's *Mémoires, ou Essais sur la musique* of 1797. Schubart's celebrated table entitled 'Characteristics of the Keys' was enormously influential on later musicians and drew comment from both Beethoven and Schumann. For Schubart, A major included 'declarations of innocent love; satisfaction with one's state of affairs; hope of seeing one's beloved again when parting; youthful cheerfulness and trust in God'. The autumnal quality which many commentators have ascribed to both Mozart's Quintet and Concerto arises in part from the use of a solo instrument which was commonly regarded as gentle and melancholy within a key which, for a variety of psychological and physical reasons, was generally thought to be brilliant and lively. Only in the nineteenth century did writers consider the implications of such a paradox for key characteristics as a whole.[4] In the event, the A clarinet was chosen as a solo instrument by relatively few composers between Mozart and Brahms.[5]

The age of virtuosity

The early years of the nineteenth century were a glorious period in the history of the clarinet and its repertory. In an age devoted to virtuosity the clarinet achieved a natural pre-eminence among wind instruments, whilst at the same time lending an important tone-colour to the Romantic orchestral palette. Clarinet quartets and quintets continued to be popular, and were usually written in *concertante* style, with the clarinet treated as soloist. From Vienna there were quartets by Leopold Kozeluch, Franz Krommer (a total of five) and Peter von Winter, usually for B♭ clarinet. One of the most integrated works is the Clarinet Quartet in E♭ (1808) by Hummel, whose string parts carry much of the interest, and whose second movement is entitled 'La seccatura' ('the nuisance'), containing different time-signatures for each of the players. Of clarinettist-composers for the medium, Bernhard Crusell takes pride of place with his three imaginative quartets

3

Opp. 2, 4 and 7, which achieved publication by Peters in Leipzig, no mean feat for a Swedish composer. Among clarinet quintets is the Op. 8 by Haydn's pupil Sigismund Neukomm, colourfully described by Cobbett as 'gifted with fatal fluency'.[6] Classical in style with some fluent part-writing, its finale comprises a set of variations on the Ukrainian folk-tune *Schöne Minke*, which became popular in Vienna *c.* 1818 and attracted variations in other genres by both Beethoven and Hummel. Virtuoso clarinettists played an important part in the development of the clarinet quintet, both as composers and performers. The Nuremberg clarinettist Heinrich Backofen was unusual in opting for a quartet of violin, two violas and cello, following the example of Mozart's Horn Quintet. This instrumentation recurs in the quintets by Krommer and Andreas Romberg. The latter is a substantial piece published in 1821, which transcends the vogue for mere virtuosity. As both performer and composer, Heinrich Baermann was a seminal influence upon the genre, writing clarinet quintets with virtuoso solo parts, of which Op. 23 in E flat includes an emotive Adagio long attributed to Wagner. Baermann also inspired Meyerbeer to compose his Clarinet Quintet in E flat, written in Vienna in 1813. Its central movement is remarkably evocative of the 'Sylvana' Variations Op. 33 for clarinet and piano by Weber, whose close association with Baermann also produced two concertos, a concertino and the Quintet Op. 34.[7]

Weber's Clarinet Quintet was to find a place in the clarinet repertory alongside the quintets by Mozart and Brahms, although it is a fundamentally different type of work, transferring Baermann's brilliant virtuosity from the concerto to a chamber context.[8] Technical virtuosity extends over the entire compass of the instrument, but the Fantasia movement combines an exploration of the clarinet's cantabile qualities with a wide-ranging expressive vocabulary which is overtly theatrical. Baermann's specialities of slurred leaps and fluent chromatic scales are given due prominence. The strings contribute occasional dramatic touches, and are assigned an important imitative episode in the finale. Another Quintet which retains a foothold in the repertory is Antonín Reicha's Op. 89 in B flat, dating from *c.* 1820. Reicha had probably heard Mozart's Quintet in Vienna before he moved to Paris in 1808 and may well have intended his own work for Jacques Jules Bouffil, professor at the Paris Conservatoire and a member of the wind quintet for which Reicha wrote as many as twenty-four pieces. Reicha's Quintet can hardly be compared with Weber's, though it contains some melodic, harmonic and rhythmic interest, to which the strings as well as the clarinet contribute. Another French example of the period is the clarinet quintet by Rodolphe Kreutzer.

Virtuoso chamber music for clarinet mirrored a burgeoning concerto repertory. In addition to Weber, Crusell and Spohr contributed expressive virtuoso examples, expanding the range of solo idioms in a variety of ways. The power and strength of the B♭ clarinet in the vast majority of these works contrasts markedly with the effect of Mozart's writing for A clarinet; Spohr's unusual choice of the A for his Fourth Concerto in E minor evokes a quite different sound-world from other concertos of the period. In his Concerto Mozart had elevated the soloist to a position of new importance (despite the inherent sophistication of his orchestral writing), which the Romantic generation went on to exploit in their different ways. Weber's F minor Concerto was another of the works in which Brahms heard Mühlfeld; it explores a sound-world quite new at its period, blending instrumental effect with the overtly operatic.

A context for clarinet writing of a more integrated kind was the large body of chamber music for mixed wind and string ensemble, initiated by Beethoven's Septet Op. 20. The composer's eventual irritation at the work's continuing popularity has been well documented, but among its many devotees was Heinrich Baermann, who quoted the clarinet solo in the Adagio at the head of his contribution to Gustav Schilling's *Beethoven Album* of 1846, with the remark:

> I was always profoundly moved when I played the above wonderful part. I thought I heard the swan song of the immortal master, and am convinced that the artist who manages to perform this beautiful motif with the intimacy and warmth which Beethoven thought and felt, will grip and inspire every listener. He will elucidate the greatness of that man who effected such indescribable magic with so few notes, and who knew how to arouse the tenderest regions of the soul.[9]

Schubert's Octet, another six-movement work in the divertimento tradition, was clearly modelled on the Beethoven. There were septets from this period by lesser composers such as Conradin Kreutzer and

Friedrich Witt, as well as a minor masterpiece by the Swedish composer Franz Berwald.

Chamber works involving clarinet and piano also produced some well-integrated textures. Weber's *Grand Duo Concertant* Op. 48 of 1816 revolutionised the medium at a stroke, introducing a theatrical element to both instrumental parts and demanding from both players a great deal more than mere instrumental technique. Another significant contribution is the *Duo* Op. 15 by the tragically short-lived Norbert Burgmüller. There were also well-written and idiomatic sonatas by the young Mendelssohn and by Franz Danzi. Beethoven's Trio Op. 11 (with cello) is an important precursor of Brahms's Op. 114, and he also explored this medium in his arrangement of the Septet, Op. 38. Amongst other composers for this combination around 1810 were Beethoven's pupil Archduke Rudolph and also Ferdinand Ries. The genre survived to the middle of the century at the hands of a few minor composers, a set of three trios Opp. 56, 60 and 63 by Gaetano Corbicello being published *c.* 1840. A Trio Op. 2 in E flat by František Jan Škroup dates from 1846, contemporary with Karl Vollweiler's *Trio on Italian Themes* Op. 15. Far more significant than any of these was Schumann's set of *Märchenerzählungen* Op. 132 (1853), which follows Mozart's trio combination of clarinet and piano with viola rather than cello.

Clarinet chamber music after 1850

During the second half of the century chamber music was still regarded by some as barely accessible to the layman: 'an appearance of being intimately familiar with it bestows an aura of an exceptional musicality and thus fosters affectation, snobbery and hypocrisy'.[10] Theodor Helm, who came to admire Bruckner's music in the 1880s, witnessed the first performances in 1892 of both his Eighth Symphony and Brahms's Clarinet Quintet. Describing the latter as masterly, he nevertheless wrote in the *Deutsche Zeitung* of 28 December: 'What does even the most beautiful "chamber piece" signify – a genre that is effective only in a small space and therefore addresses itself to narrow circles – in comparison with a symphony like the latest by Bruckner, whose thrillingly all-powerful tonal language ... is capable of inspiring thousands upon thousands who have ears to hear and a heart to hear what is heard.'

For the solo clarinettist of the second half of the century there continued an avalanche of virtuoso pieces such as operatic fantasias and pot-pourris designed to display the performer's virtuosity. But by mid-century the earlier flood of wind concertos had already slowed to a trickle. Politically, many of the small courts were being absorbed into larger duchies or kingdoms, with a consequent loss in the number of orchestras available. Socially, the clarinet was becoming more accessible to a wider cross-section of the general public, more an instrument of the drawing room or small concert hall. In terms of fashion, the musical world was by now in need of a change of colour. Hanslick may have spoken for a large element of the public when in 1870 he advised the Italian virtuoso Romeo Orsi to 'join an orchestra – that is the place where we know the value of clarinettists, flautists, oboists and bassoonists; the times are past when crowds of these wandering musicians came to give recitals on their boring little pipes.'[11] In *Grove's Dictionary* Philipp Spitta noted in 1889 that 'Wind-instruments are now out of fashion for concert playing, and one seldom hears anything on such occasions but the piano and violin, instead of the pleasing variety which used to prevail with so much advantage to art'. Writing in the 1940s Geoffrey Rendall was to characterise the whole nineteenth century as dividing roughly into two periods – fifty years of progress and fifty years of comparative stagnation, with a brief revival of interest in the clarinet in the 1890s. He observed that from the 1850s the wind player had been relegated to the position of inferiority in public estimation he had occupied until quite recently.[12]

Duos with piano from the three or four decades preceding the Brahms chamber music mainly took the form of sets of character pieces. In terms of sheer musical quality Schumann's *Phantasiestücke* Op. 73 (1849) remain pre-eminent, and they are also significant in anticipating Brahms's use of the A clarinet. There were other sets by Loewe (1850, for C clarinet), and by Gade, Reinecke, Winding, Verhey and Stanford. But the clarinet sonata enjoyed a modest revival and the genre yielded more examples at this period than is commonly realised. The Russian Ella Adaievsky's *Sonate grecque* was written in 1880, though published only in 1913.[13] From Germany Richard

Hofmann's two Sonatas Op. 48 in G and F of 1885 are now forgotten, although the ambitious Sonata Op. 38 (1888) by Felix Draesecke has recently been reprinted. There were other sonatas from Friedrich Kücken and Gustave Lange. Joseph Rheinberger published his Sonata Op. 105a in 1893, the year before Brahms's Sonatas Op. 120 were composed. From France came sonatas by Reicha's pupil Eugène Walckier (c. 1870), René de Boissdeffre (c. 1875) and in 1890 a *Sonate d'église* (with organ) by Léon Karren. The brilliant, melodramatic Sonata Op. 76 by Théodore Gouvy dates from 1882. There were several English contributions, including a Sonata in A major (1870) by Sterndale Bennett's pupil Alice Mary Smith, whose clarinet concerto was premièred at the 1872 Norwich Festival. These were written for the celebrated English clarinettist Henry Lazarus, as was a sonata by the Irishman George Osborne. A dry, unimaginative sonata by Charles Swinnerton Heap was published by Breitkopf and Härtel in 1880. Ebenezer Prout was unusual in choosing the A clarinet for his Sonata Op. 26, dedicated to Leonard W. Beddome and published c. 1890 by Augener. He shows considerable understanding of clarinet idioms, such as arpeggios, leaps and chromatic runs, as well as the clarinet's potential for cantabile, though the work's rather academic flavour has ensured its continued obscurity, notwithstanding an eloquent Largo espressivo in F sharp major. Significantly, Prout's work has an alternative version for viola, like Brahms's Sonatas Op. 120.[14] An even later example was the unpublished F minor Sonata c. 1893 by Samuel Coleridge-Taylor.

Trios with cello were more popular than clarinet quintets. A *Terzetto* Op. 175 by Franz Hünten was published in 1851. Almost as little known today is a somewhat conservative if well-crafted trio by Louise Farrenc, published in 1861. A yet later trio from 1870 is Vollweiler's *Fantaisie on Russian Airs*. In France Vincent d'Indy's Op. 29 of 1887 narrowly pre-dated Brahms's Clarinet Trio, as did Emil Hartmann's Serenade Op. 24 of 1890.[15] Activity in the field of the clarinet quintet had apparently by this time slowed to a trickle. Ludwig Pape had an Adagio published in 1863, the year also of the Clarinet Quintet Op. 44 in B flat by the violin virtuoso Theodor Täglichsbeck.[16] Much of the clarinet repertory mentioned above proved worthy rather than enduring, and thus the stage was set for the Trio, Quintet and Sonatas

composed by Brahms in the 1890s to make an incalculable contribution to the revival of the clarinet's profile as a solo instrument.

The development of the clarinet

As we have already noted, the five-keyed clarinet became established
as the standard instrument in Mozart's day, though whether this was
the configuration favoured by a virtuoso such as Stadler has not yet
been firmly established. Though a sixth key is known to have been
added to the clarinet as early as 1768, the most celebrated advocate of
an additional $c\sharp'/g\sharp''$ key was Lefèvre, whose 1802 tutor noted that
without such a mechanism $c\sharp'$ was virtually indistinguishable from d'.
In general players remained suspicious of extra keywork, because
of the increased risk of leakage. However, increased musical demands
upon the clarinet brought new attempts to render the instrument
more flexible. There were important developments in England and in
France, whilst in Germany an anonymous writer in 1808 remarked in the
Allgemeine musikalische Zeitung that at least eight keys were necessary
to avoid dull and unusable notes. Baermann employed a ten- (later
a twelve-) keyed clarinet, whilst Crusell purchased an eleven-keyed
model from the great Dresden maker Heinrich Grenser. Spohr specified in the preface to his First Concerto what extra keywork was
necessary for the solo instrument, aiming by the use of a thirteen-
rather than a five-keyed clarinet to free himself from the traditional
restrictions of the genre. Most significantly, in 1812 the player-inven-
tor Iwan Müller presented to a panel at the Paris Conservatoire a new
thirteen-keyed B♭ clarinet which he (somewhat rashly) claimed was
omnitonic. He was doubtless most disappointed that the judges,
including the composers Cherubini and Méhul, rejected the new
clarinet on the grounds that the exclusive adoption of a single instrument (and consequent abandonment of A and C clarinets) would
deprive composers of an important tonal resource. Significant in
relation to the chamber music of both Mozart and Brahms is the
adjudicators' continued differentiation between the tone-quality of
clarinets in B♭ ('propre au genre pathétique') and A ('propre au genre
pastoral'), adhering to the earlier perceptions of the instruments we
have already noted.

Despite this setback, the clarinet promoted by Müller proved to be very influential. It remains the basis for the modern German clarinet today, following interim developments by Sax, Carl Baermann and Oehler. Müller designed larger and more even-sized toneholes in the lower half of the instrument, giving a warmer sound at louder dynamic levels. Unlike some other makers, he was careful to vent the extra holes and to give special consideration to the acoustical placing of all the holes, together with convenient associated keywork. His newly designed keys had a hollow cup soldered to the end, in which was fixed a cushion-type pad of kid leather stuffed with fine wool. For the first time in its history, each tone hole on the clarinet was counter-sunk, having a rim for the pad to rest on; this has remained an important feature of clarinet design ever since.[17] Müller expressed confidence that this design would prevent leakage from the extra mechanism. In 1817 he invented the metal ligature to secure the reed, intending to replace the practice of tying it on with waxed thread or silk cord; curiously, Germany is virtually the only place in the world to have resisted this development to this day. Müller is also accredited with inventing the thumb-rest for the right hand, now universally adopted.

The move to larger toneholes exacerbated acoustical problems in the right-hand area of the clarinet, which Adolphe Sax alleviated by adding rings (or *brilles*), which allowed the three uppermost fingers effectively to control four toneholes. Excellent instruments based on this model were manufactured in Brussels by Eugène Albert and then his sons; imported into England in large numbers these so-called 'simple-system' clarinets were displaced only in the inter-war years.[18] In Germany the clarinet continued to develop. Richard Mühlfeld used the system developed by Carl Baermann, which in essence was Müller's model with a number of additions.[19] Sax's right-hand rings were supplemented by a left-hand set, but the principal enhancement was the provision of alternative levers and touch-pieces, to aid technical fluency. After Baermann the instrument was modified principally by the Berlin clarinettist and maker Oskar Oehler and his design constitutes the modern German clarinet; it has few differences in fingering from its predecessor, but considerably more toneholes to provide a complex network of venting.[20] As Nicholas Shackleton has observed, it is only recently that theoretical understanding has been gained of the disadvantages of designing an instrument with an excessive number of toneholes.[21] It was finally during Mühlfeld's lifetime that boxwood gave way to the denser blackwoods as the principal material for clarinet manufacture, though he remained faithful to his boxwood instruments until his death in 1907.

These German designs contrast markedly with the Boehm system which gradually came into use elsewhere, even though they borrowed some of its particular mechanical features. The Boehm system was devised by the clarinettist Hyacinthe Klosé with the maker Auguste Buffet *jeune* and was first exhibited in 1843. This clarinet required a major change of fingering, since its basic *c''* major scale is played simply by raising successive fingers, eliminating some previously significant 'forked' fingerings because of their reduced venting. Another significant advance was the complex set of interlocking levers for the little fingers, which greatly reduced the frequency with which it is necessary to slide from one key to another, whilst providing previously unavailable trills. Today's distinction between French and German traditions of clarinet technique and manufacture was already in place, and in terms of tone-quality as well as mechanical details Mühlfeld's clarinets were quite different from the Boehm instrument with which we are now familiar. An excellent characterisation of the German tradition appears in Brymer (*Clarinet*, pp. 150–4). The German school, he observes, produces

> a clarinet tone of a very considerable purity; a compact sound which can sustain a very beautiful *legato*. To players used to overcoming much less resistance [than the stiff German reed] it is astonishing how the best German players can support long phrases and achieve such a wide range of dynamics ... It is a gentle, edgeless sound which only at very close quarters has anything of a wind-hiss audible in it ... The whole background is one of great expressiveness and vocal style ... The finest German players are not only highly accomplished, but superbly and traditionally trained to become highly artistic performers.

Mühlfeld's Baermann–Ottensteiner clarinets

Carl Baermann (1810–85) was a member of the Munich court orchestra during Theobold Boehm's presence there as a flautist, where he must have observed his development of the flute. Brahms met Baermann in 1874 whilst giving some concerts in Munich; he presented him with the autograph of *Phänomen*, from the duets for female voices with piano Op. 61.[22] It was about 1860 that Baermann collaborated with the Munich maker Georg Ottensteiner (1815–79) on his new clarinets.[23] Having worked in Paris and in his birth place Füssen, Ottensteiner moved to Munich in 1851; Baermann claimed to have persuaded him to do this. In view of Ottensteiner's experience in Paris, it is perhaps not surprising that his 1860 price-list includes the Boehm system among several other models of clarinet.[24] Among his commissions were sets of new flat-pitch wind and brass instruments for the Munich Royal Opera, which he supplied in 1867 at a cost of 2834 gulden.[25] Apart from the evidence of Mühlfeld's instruments themselves, Baermann's *Vollständige Clarinett-Schule* (Offenbach, 1864–75) is the most useful source of information about these clarinets. This tutor achieved a very wide circulation during Baermann's lifetime and afterwards. Baermann remarked that his criteria for an unbiased appraisal of any new design were that the character of the instrument should not be adversely affected and that existing positive features should not be sacrificed. The configuration of his mechanism is tabulated in Appendix 3. Baermann remarked that no clarinet could play perfectly in tune, but that every musician knows that c♯ as the major third of A is distinguishable from d♭ as the minor third of B flat minor. It was rare for such enharmonic distinctions to play a part in clarinettists' discourse, though they were taken for granted in the major eighteenth-century flute treatises by Quantz and Tromlitz. When Mühlfeld's clarinets were recently examined, they were indeed found to have excellent intonation; furthermore, 'the overall effect is a most beautiful warm tone, just what one would hope to discover at the source of Brahms's inspiration'.[26]

2

Brahms and the orchestral clarinet

Brahms's orchestras

Brahms must have experienced the playing of various clarinettists, since a number of different centres became associated with the premières of his orchestral works, including Vienna (Opp. 50, 56a, 73, 81, 90), Hamburg (Opp. 12, 13, 16), Karlsruhe (Opp. 54, 55, 68), Leipzig (Opp. 45, 77) and Hanover (Opp. 11, 15). In the current climate of interest in late nineteenth-century performance practice it is significant that these orchestras varied considerably in size during the period in which Brahms was composing orchestral music. In the Leipzig Gewandhaus orchestra (which Mendelssohn had directed during the 1830s) the woodwind personnel numbered approximately ten players *c*. 1844. By 1881 it had increased to fifteen, with the addition of another oboe, clarinet and bassoon, as well as cor anglais, bass clarinet and contrabassoon.[1] This orchestra as a whole totalled between fifty and sixty players during the time of Schumann's association. But as late as 1864, the Düsseldorf orchestra, which Schumann had previously conducted, numbered only thirty-four players. In 1859 Richard Wagner reported, 'I am not aware that the number of permanent members of an orchestra has, in any German town, been rectified according to the requirements of modern instrumentation'. Written after hearing the Meiningen orchestra under von Bülow in 1884, a report by the critic Eduard Hanslick suggests that the orchestra's forty-eight players placed it at a disadvantage by comparison with the ninety-strong Vienna Philharmonic. However, Hanslick was not blind to the possible advantages of a smaller group, writing of the 'most admirable discipline' with which von Bülow had 'transformed it [the orchestra] into an instrument upon which he produces nuances possible only with a discipline to which larger orchestras would not ordinarily submit'.[2] Indeed, Brahms himself favoured the more intimate blend available at Meiningen, as a letter from von Bülow to Richard Strauss in 1886 testifies.

The character of the orchestral clarinet

During Brahms's lifetime commentators on the clarinet were fulsome in their praise of the instrument. Writing in Hamburg in mid-century, Robert Vollstedt reported, 'The clarinet is not only the finest wind instrument in the orchestra, but also the one with the widest range. The sound of the clarinet is closest to the human voice. What a wealth of resources composers have here to achieve the finest effects.'[3] In his treatise of 1843 Berlioz displayed an intimate knowledge of the clarinet, the different pitches available and the individual qualities of each of the registers. His division of the clarinet into four registers – low, chalumeau, medium and high – and subsequent advice on how best to write for each, corresponds with Brahms's own treatment of the instrument.[4] Gevært's treatise of 1885 echoes the sentiments of Vollstedt:

> No wind instrument offers to the composer such manifold technical possibilities as the clarinet ... [with its] wide compass and diverse tone-colours ... [and] flexibility in the expression of dynamic nuances ... Its tone is soft, yet incisive ... [and] it adjusts itself admirably to the various forms of musical thought: an expressive interpreter of solemn song, the clarinet deals easily and naturally with fluent passages, so long as they are not too far removed from its most usual keys.[5]

From the remarks of Carl Baermann can be discerned something of the sound of the clarinet of Brahms's era. When well played it can achieve such close similarity to a fine singing voice, by virtue of its beauty of tone, which enables the performer to speak to the heart:

> The finer the tone, the more poetic the effect. The tone is fine when it has a full, vibrant, metallic sound, and retains the same characteristics at all volumes and in all registers, when the tone does not deteriorate at full strength, and does not leave a piercing impression; when it is so expressive and flexible that it can perform all the notes lightly and smoothly in the quiet passages – in a word, when it resembles a superla-

tively fine and full soprano voice. If this register (the best on the clarinet) is fine-toned, then the lower notes will of themselves also be so, and one is on the right track. But even if the tone possesses all those characteristics and lacks inner life – the 'divine spark' intrinsic to man as a guarantee of his destiny, 'the soul' – then all effort and striving is of no avail, for this frigid music cannot be touched by the fire of Prometheus.[6]

The German tradition of wind writing

As a composer of orchestral music, Brahms quite naturally drew upon the heritage of his nineteenth-century predecessors Beethoven, Schubert, Mendelssohn and Schumann. Where Beethoven's oeuvre reflects his growing affection towards the orchestral clarinet, Brahms seems to have been innately aware of the instrument's potential, as is evident in his earliest orchestral music. He seems from the outset to have shared Beethoven's mature fondness for the combination of clarinets and bassoons with or without horns, representative of the 'warmer and round-toned blends' available by excluding an oboe sonority.[7]

It has recently been remarked upon how well suited the woodwind ensemble of four pairs was to the Viennese Classical style, 'with its emphasis on leading or subsidiary part-movement in parallel thirds or sixths' offering a 'wealth of solo timbres and adequate potential for blending in skilled hands'.[8] Brahms's special fondness for such writing places him firmly within this tradition. There are of course many textural parallels with earlier composers, such as the antiphonal treatment of wind and strings which occurs in the first movements of Schubert's Sixth Symphony and Brahms's First Symphony. The finale of his Sixth Symphony illustrates Schubert's writing for pairs of winds in parallel thirds, often at the distance of an octave, another hallmark of Brahms's orchestral style. The celebrated oboe and clarinet doubling in the opening of the Symphony No. 8 in B minor, a combination also used in the first two movements of his Symphony No. 9, contrives to achieve a blend by virtue of the instruments' proximity within the orchestra. When Brahms wishes to blend clarinet and oboe, especially in his later works, he again takes Schubert as a model. The archetypal manner in which upper-register oboe and clari-

15

net share solos in the second subject of the Andante con moto of Schubert's Ninth is also heard in the symphonic music of Brahms, for example in the passage from bar 38 in the Andante sostenuto of his First Symphony.

Within Mendelssohn's innovative orchestration it is the clarinet writing and overall wind scoring in the overtures and incidental music that is particularly characteristic. One of the hallmarks of this technique is his predilection for chamber textures, where winds are often isolated within the context of a smaller number of forces, as in the incidental music for *A Midsummer Night's Dream* and the overture to *The Hebrides*. The maintenance of a distinction between wind, strings and brass is also a feature of Mendelssohn's symphonic style. Individual movements, such as the Adagio of the 'Scottish Symphony', seem particularly premonitory of Brahms. Schumann's powerful handling of the clarinet in his orchestral music was undoubtedly another important influence on Brahms. It is significant that Brahms expressed a preference for the more opaque first version of what is commonly known as Schumann's Symphony No. 4.[9]

Brahms and the clarinet: early works

In a number of important ways the two serenades (written during 1857 and 1858) bear witness to Brahms's early appreciation of the Austro-German symphonic tradition of clarinet writing. Many of the idioms which were expanded and exploited in Brahms's late clarinet music under the influence of Richard Mühlfeld were part of his means of musical expression from the outset. Whilst his serenades place Brahms firmly within the tradition of Classical chamber music, they subsume in miniature the hallmarks of his orchestral style. The Serenade No. 1, which existed in three versions before publication in its present form in 1860, was inspired by 'the exceptional qualifications of the wind performers' in the Detmold court orchestra.[10] Brahms follows tradition in his scoring for clarinets in pairs but also writes much for the first player which is soloistic and often associated with the melodic material assigned to the horn, as at the beginning of the piece. The opening of the Adagio especially shows his understanding of the emotional power of the clarinet. A wind-trio texture towards the end of its development makes a feature of two clarinets and bassoon, a classical coloration which recurs in Trio I. The timbral similarity between the codas of movements I and III is hardly accidental; in both contexts Brahms pairs clarinets underneath solo flute with minimal lower string accompaniment. The treatment of oboes and clarinets as alternatives outside tutti textures may readily be traced back through the early Romantics to Mozart. In Brahms's Second Serenade all five movements begin with a distinguishable clarinet sonority. The work's opening features clarinets and bassoons in combination, and this soon develops into a *Harmonie* colour, with clarinets occasionally replaced by the oboes. Even more significant is the wide range of idiomatic writing in the third movement, Adagio non troppo. For example, the wide leaps between chalumeau and upper registers which characterise the solo from bar 42 might be seen as prophetic of similar writing within Brahms's late clarinet chamber music, especially the F minor Sonata Op. 120 no. 1; the accompanying figuration in the second clarinet is similarly idiomatic. In the finale the ingenious textural isolation of clarinets and bassoons in thirds and movement in contrary motion (bars 54–74 and 290–300) identifies the works within a genuine serenade tradition, to which his clarinet sonorities seem especially well suited.

Among Brahms's earliest compositions with voices and instruments is *Begräbnisgesang* Op. 13 for mixed choir, twelve winds and timpani, written in 1858 and premièred the following year. With its rich scoring for oboes, clarinets, bassoons, horns, trombones, tuba and timpani, *Begräbnisgesang* belongs to a certain well-established tradition of funeral music. In the light both of his 1855 letter to Clara Schumann, extolling the virtues of the combination of basset-horns and human voice,[11] and of our knowledge of Brahms's musicological interests, it is likely that Brahms was familiar with and consequently influenced by Mozart's *Maurerische Trauermusik* K477/479a. Brahms's work contains some highly idiomatic clarinet writing, especially in combination with horns and bassoons; an arpeggiated accompaniment in the chalumeau register (bars 49–57, 76–84) is in the finest Classical traditions of this texture.

Mature orchestral writing

The clarinet within the Harmonie

Contemporary with the serenades and equally essential to an under-standing of the development of Brahms's orchestral writing is the First Piano Concerto, completed in 1858.[12] His use of the clarinet in this work is subtle; not treating it as an important solo voice, he none the less enfolds it effectively within various wind combinations. Brahms's fondness for a *Harmonie* texture is evident during the expo-sition (bars 176–81), with clarinets in characteristic sixths above a bassoon pedal whilst flute and oboe engage in melodic imitation. In the recapitulation (bars 400–5) Brahms omits the oboe, placing the sixths in flutes and bassoon; clarinets provide the melody in the extreme upper register and a chalumeau pedal. Throughout the concerto is retained the characteristic tendency for clarinet and oboe to be viewed as alternatives within the *Harmonie*. The two instruments appear alternately as the upper voices of a wind texture and there is once more a special relationship of clarinets and bassoons.

The coupling of clarinets with horns and bassoons is a recurrent texture within Brahms's symphonic movements, beginning with the Un poco allegretto e grazioso of the First Symphony, whose opening clarinet melody can surely be regarded as a precursor of the Andantino of the Clarinet Quintet. The Andante of the Third Symphony pre-sents an effective blend of the same combination, whilst the Andante moderato of the Fourth Symphony displays a mature, sophisticated blend of these forces, music clearly in the tradition of the Larghetto of Beethoven's Second Symphony.

Although tutti woodwind writing is common throughout the sym-phonies, the combination of flutes, clarinets and bassoons held a spe-cial attraction for Brahms, as illustrated by the answering phrase (bar 11) of the aforementioned third movement of the First Symphony, the opening of the Second Symphony and many other examples. Another significant *Harmonie* texture comprises solo oboe above pairs of clari-nets and bassoons. The Allegretto grazioso of the Second Symphony adds pizzicato cellos to evoke a genuine serenade effect. A related example of different character is the celebrated oboe solo which opens the Adagio of Brahms's Violin Concerto, where the accompanying winds are flutes, clarinets, horns and bassoons. On both occasions the first clarinet emerges effectively to share the limelight. Finally in the first movement of the Third Symphony may be noted a new sonority at bars 64–8, 173–7 and 195–8, with a single melodic thread in wood-wind octaves, each pair à 2.[13]

The chalumeau register

Brahms's confident use of the chalumeau register in the Clarinet Quintet is anticipated by a large number of orchestral contexts, an early example being the finely scored wind chord (with the two clarinets lying beneath the bassoon) which accompanies the opening subject of the First Piano Concerto. Chording involving low clarinets recurs in the scherzo of the Fourth Symphony (bars 177ff), a move-ment which also has some solo motifs in this register (bars 282ff).[14] In solo writing within the third movement of the First Symphony the arpeggiated countermelody at bar 19 incorporating upper and chalu-meau registers seems related to contexts in the later chamber music. In the Third Symphony the linking of arpeggiated figures including the chalumeau register may also be observed in the first movement (bars 51ff, 160ff) and in the third (bar 39). The German Requiem anticipates some of these solo contexts, with especially effective use of the chalumeau register as accompaniment during the fourth movement (bars 24–46, 108–23).[15] A characteristic chalumeau figuration is also used under the horn solo at bars 100–4 of the Andante sostenuto of the First Symphony.

Solos and special effects

The effectiveness of a solo clarinet at the quiet ending of a movement, which is such an important feature of the Quintet, is foreshadowed by the stunningly evocative falling phrase which concludes the Adagio non troppo of the Second Symphony. Clarinet solos are also featured near to the quiet endings of Brahms's slow movements to the Third and Fourth Symphonies. The sensuous aspect of the instrument's character is often exploited in other contexts, for example in the clarinet thirds at bar 35 within the middle section of the same movement. The opening of the fourth movement of the *German Requiem* finds flute and clarinet moving seductively in octaves, whilst the equally common combination of clarinet and bassoon finds eloquent expression on a large number of occasions, for example in the Andante of the Third Symphony (bars 40ff).[16] This work's first movement has a second subject (bars 36ff) which comprises a nicely judged clarinet solo around the 'break' of the instrument, accompanied by flute, bassoon and lower strings. On several occasions the prominence of clarinets is indicative of a true chamber texture, as in the lyrical (and demanding) passage *più adagio* in bars 59–64 of the Andante of the Second Piano Concerto, where the dialogue in the two winds is accompanied by the soloist, just prior to the recapitulation of the opening cello melody. Finally, the exquisite texture of clarinet and violin in octaves, which plays such a prominent part in the Quintet, is anticipated in the Adagio non troppo of the Second Symphony (bars 38–9), at the recapitulation to the first movement of the Violin Concerto (bars 393–7) and in the Andante of the Double Concerto (bars 38–45).

As we have observed, Brahms was sensitive to the clarinet's orchestral potential from an early stage in his career. He seems immediately to have appreciated its versatility and the different character of its registers. Though the discussions with Mühlfeld late in his life surely expanded his technical knowledge of the instrument, the confidence with which he handled the orchestral clarinet from the time of the Serenades onwards provided a secure base from which to discover yet more of the instrument's potential. Indeed, Brahms's ability to write idiomatically for the clarinet was far more established by the early 1890s than most writers have been willing to acknowledge. Mühlfeld's achievement was to unleash further potential for Brahms's creativity via the clarinet, which would otherwise have inevitably remained unrealised.

3

Brahms's chamber music before 1891

Aspects of style

Brahms was involved with chamber music from his childhood years. He played in a private subscription concert organised by his father as early as 1843, in which the programme included Beethoven's Quintet Op. 16 and one of Mozart's piano quartets.[1] In 1851 two of his own chamber works were played at a private concert, and it was as a chamber music player and composer that Brahms introduced himself to Vienna in 1862 with the piano quartets Opp. 25 and 26. He continued to perform in this capacity, eventually partnering Mühlfeld in the clarinet sonatas at the end of his life.

Brahms's chamber masterpieces, listed in Appendix 1, began with the Piano Trio in B, Op. 8, whose first public performance took place in New York in 1855. Throughout Brahms's life, the traditional medium of chamber music was – paradoxically – often a vehicle for his newest ideas. In the early 1860s,

> Brahms's strong concern with chamber music at this period of his creative life was partly a product of his profound disquiet at the stylistic developments of the 'new German School', particularly at the symphonic poems of Liszt. While chamber music had a traditional, even conservative, role in the genre-system of these times, it contained within itself an importantly progressive stylistic aspect. That 'thematic density' which formed one of the most significant stylistic continuities from Beethoven through Brahms to Schoenberg found its most characteristic home in chamber music; and the textural dialogue so fundamental to the genre, gave possibilities of great flexibility and intensity in thematic manipulation which were particularly congenial to Brahms.[2]

As examples of this modernity, Robert Pascall instances the melody at the opening of the G major String Sextet Op. 36, the harmonic nuance

21

of the third movement of the C minor String Quartet Op. 51 no. 1, and the formal originalities in the third movement of the C major Piano Trio Op. 87 and the second of the F major String Quintet Op. 88.[3] The chamber music is to some extent autobiographical, in that we may observe in it much about Brahms's relationship to his predecessors, his central musical concerns and his development as a composer. Pascall observes that Brahms built most obviously not on the work of Mendelssohn and Schumann but on that of Beethoven and Schubert:

> It is possible to view his music as an integration of the Haydn–Beethoven tradition of dynamic argument and dramatic power with the Mozart–Schubert tradition of relaxed lyricism and serene beauty. Brahms seems a more sensuous composer than Beethoven both in matters of texture and melody, and a more dynamically symphonic composer than Schubert; the ethos is more strenuous, more Protestant, more North German.

Pascall proceeds to compare the B flat String Sextet Op. 18 with Schubert's last piano sonata D. 960, and the Piano Quintet Op. 34 with Beethoven's F minor Quartet Op. 95. It scarcely needs emphasising that the lyrical vein coupled with dramatic and structural power becomes an important feature of the Clarinet Quintet. Hungarian elements (as well as German folksong) began to be incorporated in the early 1860s in the first two piano quartets and the Piano Quintet.

Formal procedures

Within individual movements, Brahms's formal procedure is often complex, as in the first movement of the F minor Clarinet Sonata, where sonata combines with variation. Brahms told his only formal composition student, Gustav Jenner, to examine the sonata forms of Beethoven, paying particular attention to the influence of a theme on the design of a movement. He also encouraged Jenner to compare Beethoven with Schubert in this regard. From Brahms, Jenner learned that a sonata structure must grow logically from a theme, that 'one has not written a sonata if one holds together a few ideas merely with the outward form of a sonata; on the contrary, the sonata form must of necessity result from the idea'.[4] What mattered to Brahms, Jenner reports, was the spirit, not the schema, of sonata form. Brahms's preoccupation with thematic unification may be found in the cross-quotations in the first, third and fourth movements of the Clarinet Quintet. Forms based on the principle of contrast (such as ternary and rondo) tend to have thematic links between sections, as in the central movements of the Quintet. As has often been observed, his textures as well as forms are complex; unlike Classical composers who based their chamber output around a nucleus of one or two central groupings, Brahms had none such. Within the different ensembles, the instruments themselves help to generate, shape and colour the ideas. Brahms always used the textural possibilities of his instrumentation to articulate and enhance the musical argument.

Although there were marked changes in genre, form and harmony during Brahms's creative life, it is his treatment of melody which Pascall identifies as embodying the principal phases of self-consciousness, establishment and contemplation. He notes an increasing distinction in the quality of melodic writing and ever more meaningful developments of the themes themselves:

> As Brahms's life progressed, more and more notes have more and more significance, until in the last period we may speak of a melodic density different in kind from those of earlier periods. The continual intensity of melodic beauty becomes overwhelming, and such movements as the first of the second clarinet sonata show a fusion of melodic presentation and development unrivalled in Brahms and elsewhere.[5]

Chamber music with wind

Brahms's Horn Trio Op. 40 is of special significance to students of the clarinet works because it represents his only earlier engagement with a wind instrument in the context of chamber music. Just as Beethoven had found the piano and the string quartet the most flexible and congenial vehicles for his innermost ideas, so was Brahms naturally drawn to these same instruments. Whereas the genres of clarinet sonata, trio and quintet had at least been established by earlier composers, the combination of horn, violin and piano had no precedent, and even Beethoven's Horn Sonata (which Brahms knew and played) is only distantly related in character. Brahms's horn part was inspired by his principal player at Detmold, August Cordes, whose rich, mellow tone drew from Brahms enthusiastic expressions of admiration. Completed in 1865, more than quarter of a century before the Clarinet Trio and Quintet, the Horn Trio illustrates his preoccupation at that time with orchestral colouring, in which the horn plays such a significant role. The Trio was specifically intended for the valveless *Waldhorn*, which Brahms preferred to the technologically more advanced *Ventilhorn*. The characterful and atmospheric sound of the natural horn lends the work a Romantic palette outside the range of the conventional piano trio, and to complement this Brahms succeeded in making a virtue of the limitations in the horn's available notes. This intimate understanding of its possibilities is already evident in the Op. 17 songs, published in 1862 and scored for three female voices, two horns and harp. Brahms's horn writing foreshadows his later appreciation of the special qualities of the clarinet which, though more agile, requires similarly sympathetic treatment. The very opening theme of the Horn Trio remains a potent Romantic symbol, quintessential horn music in its deeply poetic vein. Throughout the work there is no hint that the absence of the flexibility, agility and versatility of other instruments is in any sense a handicap. Principal themes throughout the Trio are adapted to the harmonic series, with economical use of extremes of tessitura and sensitive accommodation of stopped notes. Brahms himself recognised the natural chiaroscuro of open and closed notes, remarking that if the player were not compelled to blend his open and stopped notes he would never learn to blend his tone in chamber music at all.[6] The horn also influences the rhythmic character of much of the material, Brahms taking advantage of its natural weightiness for the purposes of accentuation.

Even the form of the work is affected by the natural horn. Exceptionally, the sonata principle is not used in the first movement, but is replaced by a sectional plan: the reflective principal theme is presented three times in varying keys and settings, interspersed with a more restless subordinate theme, *poco più animato*. In this way, the monumental main subject is given space to breathe and expand. Both scherzo and finale are permeated by striking thematic material inspired by hunting horn idioms, whereas the intervening Adagio mesto is widely regarded as one of the most profoundly felt and one of the most subtle of all Brahms's slow movements.[7] Its melancholy mood anticipates elements in the Clarinet Trio and Quintet, and towards its close is a clear anticipation of the main theme of the finale which follows it, foreshadowing cyclic elements in the Clarinet Quintet.

Brahms's espousal of the natural horn – against the trend of his progressive contemporaries – is of special interest in today's 'historically aware' climate. Almost forty years after Brahms's death, it was still felt by at least one sympathetic writer that to write freely for the valve horn (as if it were a flute or clarinet) was to impoverish the nature of the instrument, and that to write sentimental chromatic passages shows composers forgetful of its history, its character, its style and its very personality.[8] By contrast, the Trio was roundly criticised in the Leipzig *Allgemeine musikalische Zeitung* in the New Year of 1867, following a performance on 15 December by Clara Schumann, violinist Ferdinand David and the horn player Friedrich Gumbert.[9] The *AmZ* reviewer was its then editor, the conservative composer and critic Selmar Bagge, who allowed that the work 'deeply grips the heart and fantasy', but disliked its gloom and its rhythmic weakness. He even felt dissatisfaction with the very sound of the work, which he reckoned might have been improved had Brahms used a clarinet rather than a horn. Comparing the work with Beethoven (his idol), Bagge was unconditional only in his enthusiasm for the trio of the scherzo, which he described as truly lyrical Brahms. Posterity has scarcely endorsed Bagge's response, since the Horn Trio has found considerable favour with players and listeners alike. Indeed, by comparison, Brahms's Clarinet Trio has been rather slower to find universal acceptance.

String chamber music

Brahms composed the Clarinet Quintet at the end of a lifetime of experience of writing for strings, enriched especially by his relationship with the violinist Joseph Joachim. It was Joachim, for example, who convinced him that the Piano Quintet in F minor would be too difficult and not sufficiently effective in its original guise for strings alone. Joachim was also intimately involved with the evolution of the solo part of the Violin Concerto Op. 77 in the months leading up to its première at the beginning of 1879, though Brahms retained control of the final decisions, even those relating to violin technique. The work's finale is a rondo of gypsy bravura, which pays homage to Joachim's own 'Concerto in the Hungarian Manner'. It is significant that in the generation after Joachim no less a figure than Adolfo Betti, leader of the celebrated Flonzaley Quartet, asserted that Brahms's instinct for strings was well-nigh incomparable.[10]

Brahms's music for strings and keyboard from 1854 to 1890 comprised three piano trios, two piano quartets and a piano quintet, in addition to the three violin and two cello sonatas. String chamber music consists of the Sextets Op. 18 (published 1862) and Op. 36 (1866), the Quartets Op. 51/1 and 2 (1873) and Op. 67 (1876), and the Quintets Op. 88 (1883) and Op. 111 (1891). If the sextets show an affinity in their sonority with the orchestral serenades, the works with piano are altogether more symphonic. The F minor Piano Quintet Op. 34 represents an especially intense unification of his lyrical and dynamic impulse. MacDonald has noted that one of the principal forces behind the work's tension is the extent to which its very varied materials are dominated by the interval of a minor second, the rise or fall of which 'has always been among music's most graphic metaphors for emotional disturbance'.[11] This later proves to be a prominent feature in the Clarinet Quintet.

Brahms showed special caution in tackling the medium of the string quartet; Tovey suggested that he experienced extraordinary difficulty in reducing his massive harmony and polyphony to the limits of four solo strings. Although the quartets have been enthusiastically described as logical, advanced, eloquent and subtle, they have somehow never achieved the prominence of the other chamber music or the symphonies, maintaining at least as great a profile amongst analysts as in the concert hall. In his celebrated essay 'Brahms the progressive', Arnold Schoenberg sought to prove that Brahms was in fact 'a great innovator in the realm of musical language'.[12] His account of the principle of 'developing variation' as a thematic process takes the Andante moderato from the A minor Quartet as an illustration. Schoenberg defined the technique as 'nothing but an endless reshaping of a basic shape ... there is nothing in a piece of music but what comes from the theme, springs from it and can be traced back to it; to

26

put it still more severely, nothing but the theme itself ... The various characters and forms [arise] from the fact that variation is carried out in a number of different ways.'[13] Schoenberg further expressed a special admiration for the harmonic language of the C minor Quartet, citing an extract from the first movement at the opening of his essay 'Brahms the progressive'. Others have written of an impression of economy and of a single 'mould', arising most immediately from the thematic relationships among the four movements. It has indeed been claimed that there is not only thematic unity but a real *process* spanning the whole work, the finale lacking a true development because its material has already been extensively developed in the preceding movements. This is arguably the first work in which Brahms shows a concern for such higher-level thematic processes, rather than mere recall or transformation.[14] In the first movement of the C minor Quartet at least one commentator has found 'a high proportion of what can most kindly be called non-melodic work ... There is a shortage of telling melody combined with a good deal of sheer ungainliness.'[15] Whilst this focused, more concentrated idiom and its associated cyclical procedures anticipate certain elements in the Clarinet Quintet, Brahms's lyrical impulse returns in full measure in the later work. We may note in passing that a specific formal parallel occurs in the final variations of the B flat Quartet Op. 67, which (like the Clarinet Quintet) conclude with references to the opening of its first movement.

In the two string quintets may be observed a return to the more concerted music of the sextets, a Romantic element once again combining with formal and contrapuntal workmanship. Though usually self-deprecatory, Brahms was especially proud of the F major Quintet Op. 88, describing it to Clara Schumann as one of his finest works.

The String Quintet Op. 111

Stylistic parallels between Brahms's orchestral and chamber music may be drawn through every stage of his life, ranging through the lyrical, heroic and more abstract to an earlier preoccupation with the gypsy manner which resurfaces in the Double Concerto and in the G major String Quintet Op. 111.[16] This latter work was to have been Brahms's swansong, and in style and character is of considerable significance to students of the Clarinet Quintet. In offering the String Quintet's four-handed version in December 1890, Brahms remarked, the time has come for you to say goodbye to any further compositions of mine'.[17] Though only fifty-seven years of age, he had made his will that year and planned nothing further than the revision of existing compositions. The String Quintet's finale recalls the Gypsy Rondo of the G minor Piano Quartet, whilst elsewhere in the work a combination of Slavic feeling with German moods may be observed. As Mac-Donald has remarked, Op. 111 would have made a fittingly magisterial piece with which to sign off, showing Brahms at the very height of his inventive powers and crammed with matter to give future composers food for thought. 'Above all, there is a plasticity of ideas and a quality of bold, abandoned virtuosity in the handling of the ensemble that seem to develop from the solo writing of the double Concerto and to surpass all the other chamber music for strings alone.'[18] When the Clarinet Quintet subsequently appeared after Brahms's meeting with Mühlfeld, it proved to have much in common with the Quintet Op. 111, not least in the character of the string writing and in its gypsy associations. The two works also share a sophistication of harmonic and thematic writing and phrasing, Brahms having introduced in Op. 111 a type of equality which had previously been the preserve only of overtly contrapuntal contexts.

Illustrative of the String Quintet's advanced language is the construction of its first movement, beginning with a continuously evolving sixteen-bar structure which is without precedent in his music.[19] The powerful opening idea heralds a movement not of lyrical expansiveness but of extreme economy, the exposition ending with a fluid syncopated passage which directly anticipates the Clarinet Quintet. The development is typical of its period in featuring strong contrasts of texture and dynamic. The spirited finale combines sonata and rondo, propelling the gypsy material over a complex harmonic frame. In its hectic coda the first violin dominates proceedings with true *Zigeuner* élan, after much dancing and virtuosity. If Brahms had anything to learn from Dvořák (whose chamber music he studied closely), it might have been how to wear the academic aspects of his craft lightly, and we find this occurring pre-eminently in the string

Ex. 3.1 String Quintet Op. 111, Adagio, bars 65–9

quintets. The harmonic individuality of the slow movement (incorporating modal progressions) was at once noted by Joachim, and the orchestral effect of its impassioned middle section invites immediate comparison with the Clarinet Quintet. A quasi-cadenza for viola before the final statement of the principal material seems especially close to the idiom of the later movement (Ex. 3.1).

Correspondence between Brahms and Elisabeth von Herzogenberg gives some insight into her immediate response to the String Quintet.[20] In October 1890 (before hearing it) she compared the work with its F major predecessor as possibly greater in beauty and benignity, of a riper, sweeter vintage. She especially admired the compactness and exquisite proportions of the first movement and its clear framework, in which nothing appeared superfluous. The finale prompted her to observe that 'the person who invented it all must have felt very light-hearted. One feels you must have been celebrating – say, your thirtieth birthday!' Having heard the String Quintet in December, Frau Herzogenberg thought the central movements finest in their unity of emotion, vigour and effect. In the first movement she felt the cello giving signs of protest against the exorbitant demands made upon it:

29

I venture to think, in all humility, that a person like you ought to write nothing which is not absolutely pleasing – not only to the mind but to the ear … Show a little more clemency. Go over those places again with a soft stump, as if it were a charcoal drawing, and smear it over, tone it down a little! That high, scratchy part … near the end of the development really sounds anything but beautiful. It is so *laboured*, whereas *everything* in this movement ought to sound beautiful.

In the event, Brahms retained his original text, despite some initial doubts about ensemble balance at the opening of the piece, which nowadays tends to be regarded as vibrant and rich rather than in any sense miscalculated. Tovey noted that Joachim had gradually resolved difficulties in performance and he was fulsome in his praise of the work as an immensely powerful outburst of high spirits.[21] For another writer in the 1930s, Op. 111 occupied in some ways a supreme place in Brahms's chamber music. Mason thought that together with the D minor Violin Sonata (its immediate predecessor) it marked the high point of his achievement, 'the point after which, despite the mellow, autumnal beauty of the Clarinet Quintet, the curve begins to descend'.[22] He claimed that in all the clarinet works one is conscious of a less buoyant, a more chastened mood, a sadder, more reflective beauty, whereas in Op. 111 Brahms was at the height of his technical powers and of his zest in life. Never before had he written at once with such mastery and such buoyancy of high spirits; the work represented his last expression of full and hearty manhood. As will be evident from the many appreciations of the Clarinet Quintet cited throughout this book, Mason's appraisal has never become widely accepted.

4

The genesis and reception of the
Clarinet Quintet

Brahms and Meiningen

Richard Mühlfeld's career was centred around his membership of the Meiningen orchestra, whose special and intimate characteristics have already been remarked upon in Chapter 2. During 1880–5 Hans von Bülow did much to raise its profile and he frequently programmed Brahms's music at the internationally renowned festivals of orchestral music in the city. Brahms's personal connection with the orchestra began in 1881, when he visited Meiningen to give a performance of his Second Piano Concerto. Subsequently the duke invited Brahms frequently to the castle, where he spent Christmas as a guest in both 1887 and 1888. During von Bülow's tenure as conductor Brahms is known to have made the acquaintance of Richard Mühlfeld at a rehearsal. Edwin Evans regarded the subsequent delay before the appearance of the clarinet works as 'allowing room for considerable thought having intervened – an amount, in fact, which we can only interpret as hesitation'.[1] Furthermore, a letter to Clara Schumann of July 1891 indicates that prior to his friendship with Mühlfeld, Brahms considered that during his own lifetime the art of clarinet playing had deteriorated.[2]

However, there may in fact have been some activity during Evans's so-called period of hesitation, with even the possibility that Brahms started work on a clarinet quintet in E minor. On 14 December 1888 Brahms wrote to Clara Schumann confirming that he expected to be able come to the Frankfurt Museum for a concert on 11 January the following year:

> But why is it to be a Brahms evening this time? Neither for myself nor for anybody else is this either necessary or desirable. At all events the brutal [*grausamen*] clarionet quintet would not do. I hope for the first item they will choose some beautiful chamber-music piece...[3]

31

On 22 December Brahms wrote again to Clara, wishing her the happiest of Christmases and at the same time complaining of having to answer yet more letters from the Museum directors. He asked Clara to discuss the forthcoming concert with them directly: 'we cannot begin with the sonata, and the E minor Quintet is not suitable for the programme'. Brahms was scrupulous in destroying material he deemed unworthy of publication, and Margit McCorkle is undoubtedly justified in regarding it as an open question as to whether this quintet provided material for the B minor Clarinet Quintet he eventually completed.[4]

It was von Bülow's successor Fritz Steinbach who in March 1891 drew Brahms's attention to the playing of Richard Mühlfeld. Brahms asked to be made familiar with his repertory and discussed the nature of the clarinet with him at some length. It seems that amongst the works played to Brahms by Mühlfeld was the Mozart Clarinet Quintet and Weber's F minor Concerto; there was also some Spohr. Brahms was captivated; on 17 March he wrote to Clara Schumann, 'Nobody can blow the clarinet more beautifully than Herr Mühlfeld of this place'. He thought him the finest wind player he had ever heard, calling him the 'Nightingale of the orchestra'. In this frame of mind Brahms abandoned his projected retirement and was stimulated to compose the Clarinet Trio and Quintet in 1891 and the two Sonatas in 1894.

Richard Mühlfeld

Richard Mühlfeld's career has been the subject of recent research by Pamela Weston, whose sources include material supplied by the clarinettist's grandson.[5] Born and raised in the nearby spa town of Salzungen, from the age of ten Richard played violin and clarinet in the so-called 'cure-music', an ensemble of between eleven and twenty-five part-time players trained and led by his father Leonhard and known as the 'Klapperkasten' ('Rattletrap'). Like his three elder brothers, Richard progressed to the court orchestra at Meiningen, which he joined in 1873 as a violinist.[6] His military service involved three years (1876–9) as solo clarinettist in the band of the 32nd regiment, and he was gradually called upon to play clarinet in the orchestra. In this capacity he went with the orchestra to the Bayreuth Festival in 1876, where after a performance of the overture to *Egmont* Wagner told him, 'Young friend, continue in this way and the whole world is open to you'. At subsequent Bayreuth Festivals Mühlfeld became friends with Richard, Cosima and Siegfried Wagner and was awarded the Bavarian Gold Medal of Ludwig for his services to their Festival (the Meiningen orchestra visited each year between 1888 and 1896). In Meiningen he was invited to play as soloist for the first time in 1877, and two years later was appointed principal clarinet on the retirement (through ill-health) of Wilhelm Reif (1832–90). Weston noted that Reif composed (and conducted) a concerto for Mühlfeld in 1885,[7] and he was probably responsible for Mühlfeld's choice of Baermann-Ottensteiner clarinets. Carl Baermann had appeared as soloist with the Meiningen orchestra in 1857 and made such a favourable impression on Duke Bernhard (father of Duke Georg) that he sent Reif to Munich for lessons with Baermann.[8] Mühlfeld's choice of repertory was discerning well before his meeting with Brahms; for example, he gave the Meiningen première of the Weber Concertino in 1886.[9]

Undoubtedly, Mühlfeld was respected as an exceptional musician throughout the 1880s. Even the rather chauvinistic Austrian music critic Hanslick after a visit to Meiningen commented, 'the clarinets are good, if not equal to the Viennese'. After a Leipzig concert in March 1882, Elisabeth von Herzogenberg wrote to Brahms describing how von Bülow insisted on repeating the third movement of his C minor Symphony and praising the clarinettist. Bülow entrusted sectional rehearsals of the orchestral winds to Mühlfeld. For twenty years from 1887 he also conducted a male-voice choir (composed mainly of school teachers) and on the death of Reif in 1890 succeeded him as music director. He arranged and conducted music for the court theatre and auditioned the singers. Clearly, Mühlfeld felt that there was much musical reward in staying at Meiningen, for (as Weston has observed) several important offers of work occurred which would have taken him away, and which he decided to reject. The reasons for this are not altogether clear; the duchy of Saxe-Meiningen was small and remote, even though its orchestra was acknowledged as the finest in Germany. In 1882 Mühlfeld received an invitation to play first clarinet for the Imperial Music Society in St Petersburg; in 1885 he was wanted for the Royal Opera House in Budapest; in 1887 he was invited by Felix Mottl to Karlsruhe; in 1888 by Franz Wüllner to the Cologne Conservatoire; and in 1890 by Nikisch to the Boston Symphony.

The Clarinet Trio Op. 114

Having promised to compose some chamber works for Mühlfeld, Brahms moved in July 1891 from Vienna to his summer residence in Ischl, where he proceeded to compose the Trio and the Quintet. He announced both works in a jocular letter to the Baroness Helene von Heldburg of Meiningen, dated 25 July. Several days earlier he sent the Trio to his friend Eusebius Mandyczewski, remarking that the work was only 'the twin to a far greater folly', which he was now trying to 'coax out'.[10] Meanwhile, Mühlfeld spent the summer in Bayreuth.[11] The first private performances of both works eventually took place in Meiningen on 24 November 1891.[12]

What had Brahms learned from his exposure to Mühlfeld's playing and his repertory? His choice of the darker A clarinet for both the Trio and Quintet is surely significant; as we have already observed, it seems likely that Mühlfeld discussed the difference in tone and response between the A and B♭ clarinets, perhaps observing the relative neglect of the former in chamber music since Mozart. As Malcolm MacDonald has remarked, all four clarinet works 'offer comparatively few opportunities for displays of vertiginous bravura, but continual ones for the exercise of refined musicality, intimate expression, and beautiful tone'.[13] Like Mozart, Brahms regarded the upper register as the heart of the instrument, but also incorporated the chalumeau register in his melodic invention; indeed, the opening of the Trio traverses a range of two-and-a-half octaves. Idiomatic clarinet figuration based upon scales and arpeggios features prominently throughout the work. The first movement concludes with such a passage, highly characteristic in its wide-ranging whisperings of clarinet and cello. The trio of the Menuet introduces arpeggiated figuration in the clarinet which is at the same time idiomatic and challenging for the player.

Although Brahms rated his Trio as highly as the Quintet, it was not as well received and has continued to attract criticism ever since.[14] Indeed, there is no unanimity even as to its essential character. As

Michael Musgrave observes, 'its sardonic wisdom has never attained the popularity of the latter's lambent melancholy'.[15] Philip Radcliffe remarked that several of Brahms's friends seem actually to have preferred the Trio, perhaps because of the sobriety of its Classical restraint.[16] According to Geiringer, Mandyczewski commented that its effect was as though the instruments were in love with one another.[17] Joachim wrote to Brahms from England in April 1892 that he liked the piece better and better and expressed regret that he could not take part in it. But this response to the work was not reflected in the early biographical literature. Before enthusing about the Quintet, Florence May in 1905 remarked: 'The Clarinet Trio appears to us one of the least convincing of Brahms's works ... the inspiration of this work seems to halt, the spirit to want flexibility'.[18] Three years later, H. C. Colles concurred, asserting that the Trio suggests its origins: 'it sounds like the study of an instrument, in spite of many passages of wonderful beauty'.[19] In 1916 the amateur clarinettist Oscar Street observed that although both the Trio and Quintet had become familiar in Britain, the Trio had of late become somewhat neglected, adding that in his opinion its Adagio contained as fine music as any in the two works.[20] In 1929 Tovey remarked that the work would not have been easily eclipsed if only its finale had been pathetic in mood rather than alternately defiant, reflective and humorous.[21]

Amongst the Trio's most outspoken critics was Daniel Gregory Mason, whose book describes it as one of the weakest of all Brahms's works, 'a deep trough between the two crests of the String Quintet [Op. 111] and the Clarinet Quintet'.[22] Although he allows that in the first movement the clarinet tone-colour is beautifully used to support and intensify the sombre and serious mood, he at the same time detects a poverty, or perhaps intentional bareness of line. Mason claims that during the second group Brahms resorts to almost mechanical inversion and that all the themes 'seem to betray an unmistakable apathy of the imagination'. The opening of the Adagio is 'in the end somehow tame, somehow lacking in persuasive charm. We respect but do not love it.' The Andantino grazioso is 'tuneful to triviality and of a charm so superficial that a few hearings of it bring satiety. It has an almost Italian sinuousness of line and suavity of manner that hardly becomes Northern art ... This over-dressed tune is like the pretty peasant maiden who has spoiled herself, for a holiday at the fair, with finery and cosmetics.' In the finale, 'the rather pointless changes of meter ... are a sign not of rhythmic vitality, but of defective rhythmic control ... The impression of formulism in the treatment [of the themes] is also most unescapable.' Mason asserts that 'critics have all found themselves repelled by the school-masterish, pedantic side of Brahms ... exposed rather pitilessly by the Trio because of its lack of inspiration.' But even he detects 'a high, unyielding sincerity, a grave dignity, a kind of stoic Roman virtue'.

Some fifty years on, the Trio was ripe for reappraisal. Musgrave found 'consummate formal flexibility' in the Adagio,[23] whilst admiring the concentration and formal interest of the outer movements. Mac-Donald viewed it as in many respects the logical successor to the C minor Piano Trio, observing that 'the work's emotional range is much wider than the Quintet, and far less amenable to merely comfortable interpretations. Standing at the very end of his long line of concerted chamber music with piano, it exhibits all the resource and subtlety of his late style, further stimulated by the contrasting characters of the three instruments, which permit little of the Quintet's blended sonority.'[24] He regards the Adagio as serenely philosophical, tinged with fantasy, appearing relaxed and expansive despite its masterly compression to a mere fifty-four bars. The Andantino grazioso 'evokes the manner of the *Liebeslieder* Waltzes, but now in a complex, organic form whose sophistication quite belies the well-wined tearfulness of the opening tune'. Of Fuller Maitland's remark that this latter theme could have been written by Balfe, MacDonald tartly remarks that 'he was confusing Victorian sentimentality with German sentiment'. In the finale he finds mystery and instability even in the more cheerful passages and a 'bracing rhythmic suppleness' from the alternation of 6/8 and 2/4 bars. Peter Foster attributes the charge by May and Evans of melodic inflexibility as unfair criticism of a work whose roots lie in the *alla breve* style of imitative writing.[25]

Clarinet Quintet reception, 1891–4

The Trio and Quintet offer the last, and one of the most interesting, examples of Brahms's independence of approach to a pair of works written in close proximity, and posing similar compositional demands. The Quintet's greater impact was immediate, and it became a great favourite of Joachim. He promptly proposed that both Trio and Quintet be performed at the next Joachim Quartet concert in Berlin, a major series which previously had been confined to chamber music for strings. On 1 December Brahms wrote from Hamburg to Hanslick:

> Joachim has sacrificed the virginity of his Quartet for my newest things. Hitherto he has carefully protected the chaste sanctuary but now, in spite of all my protestations, he insists that I invade it with clarinet and piano, with trio and quintet. This will take place on the 12th of December, and with the Meiningen clarinettist.[26]

At a rehearsal on the 8th Mühlfeld had a reunion with von Bülow, and there followed a public rehearsal on the 10th, at which all seats were taken. On this occasion, and at the concert which followed on the 12th, the Adagio of the Quintet was played as an encore, following the work's instantaneous success.[27]

It is perhaps a little surprising that in Vienna both the Trio and Quintet were premièred by clarinettists other than Mühlfeld. On 17 December the Trio was played by Adalbert Syrinek, principal clarinet of the Vienna Philharmonic, with Brahms and the cellist Ferdinand Hellmesberger. On 5 January the Quintet was played by F. W. Steiner, clarinettist in Baron Albert de Rothschild's private orchestra, with the Rosé Quartet.[28] Mühlfeld performed both works in Vienna on 21 January 1892.[29] Before long he was playing the work with quartets other than the Joachim, such as the Heermann, Skalitzki and Halir. In Germany there were soon performances by clarinettists other than Mühlfeld; for example, the clarinettist Friede toured the Quintet with the Cologne violinist Gustav Holländer and his Gürzenich Quartet. In America the Kneisel Quartet introduced the Quintet to Boston (1893) and New York (1894) with the clarinettist Goldschmidt.[30]

Meanwhile, Joachim had written on 16 December to Stanford in Cambridge asking for help in securing Quintet performances with Mühlfeld, praising both the work ('one of the sublimest things he ever wrote') and the clarinettist ('a stupendous fellow'). He added that the manuscript could not be sent for an English player to practise and that besides there was so much of the gypsy style about it that no one else would find the right expression. Stanford wanted Julian Egerton to play the Brahms works in England, but Joachim remained dubious:

> Is Egerton intelligent and spirited enough for playing a piece in which there is much of a dramatic, phantastic character, that wants a great variety of tone, from *ff* to *ppp* ? Tell me, and I might try to persuade Brahms when I see him in Vienna (in a fortnight) to send a copy over. He made Mühlfeld a condition of giving the manuscript.[31]

In the event Mühlfeld travelled to London under the sponsorship of Adolph Behrens, a keen amateur musician from Richmond.

A touching vignette relating to this very period survives from Cobbett's pen, in his own article on arrangements:

> When Brahms's clarinet quintet was first issued in 1892 by Simrock, a copy of it was sent to a friend of mine, Captain A. S. Beaumont, an ardent lover of chamber music, who at once organized a performance of it at his house in Norwood, engaging [George] Clinton as clarinet and Harold Bauer (at that time a violinist and now, as everybody knows, a world-famous pianist) as first violin. Clinton, through illness, failed to put in an appearance, and Bauer, delegating the violin part to me, took the clarinet part on the viola (as arranged by Brahms himself). Thanks to his wonderful sight-reading, the performance went astonishingly well, and we all trooped, a few evenings later, to hear the work in its original form played by Mühlfeld and the Joachim Quartet.[32]

This London première took place on 28 March, after which Joachim sent a telegram to Brahms telling of its remarkable success and explaining that he had reserved the Trio for the next two concerts on 2 and 4 April: 'People can appreciate the subtle things better if they have been carried away by something mighty first of all, and have confidence in the composer'. *The Times* reviewed the London première in glowing terms (see Appendix 2). Mühlfeld gave further concerts in London on 5, 10, 12 and 17 May, appearing in Liverpool on 6 May and in Manchester on 15 May.[33]

Julian Egerton attended Mühlfeld's London première and played the work in Cambridge the following month, doubtless very differently in style. His tone was reputed to be very beautiful, with scrupulous attention to detail. The conductor Percy Buck opined that he had never heard such beautiful tone from a clarinet and that he made the most perfect sounds he had ever heard.[34] George Clinton gave another London performance in early May, which drew fierce criticism of the music from Bernard Shaw:

Only the other day I remarked that I was sure to come across Brahms' new clarionet quintet sooner or later. And, sure enough, my fate over-took me last week at Mr. G. Clinton's Wind Concert at Steinway Hall. I shall not attempt to describe this latest exploit of the Leviathan Maun-derer. It surpassed my utmost expectations: I never heard such a work in my life. Brahms' enormous gift of music is paralleled by nothing on earth but Mr Gladstone's gift of words: it is a verbosity which outfaces its own commonplaceness by dint of sheer magnitude. The first move-ment of the quintet is the best; and had the string players been on sufficiently easy terms with it, they might have softened it and given effect to its occasional sentimental excursions into dreamland. Unluck-ily they were all preoccupied with the difficulty of keeping together; and they were led by a violinist whose bold, free, slashing style, though useful in a general way, does more harm than good when the strings need to be touched with great tenderness and sensitiveness.

Mr. Clinton played the clarionet part with scrupulous care, but without giving any clue to his private view of the work, which, though it shews off the compass and contrasts the registers of the instrument in the usual way, contains none of the haunting phrases which Weber, for instance, was able to find for the expression of its idiosyncrasy. The presto of the third movement is a ridiculously dismal version of a lately popular hornpipe. I first heard it at the pantomime which was produced at Her Majesty's Theatre a few years ago; and I have always supposed it to be a composition of Mr. Solomon's. Anyhow, the street-pianos went through an epidemic of it; and it certainly deserved a merrier fate than burying alive in a Brahms quintet.[35]

Clara Schumann became acquainted with the Quintet in Paul Klengel's transcription for two pianos, and wrote to Brahms from Frankfurt on 25 January 1893 that she was spending much time studying 'this heavenly work' and was eagerly looking forward to hearing Mühlfeld perform it. On 17 March she wrote in her diary that the previous day she had at last heard the Quintet in rehearsal. 'It is a really marvellous work, the wailing clarinet takes hold of one; it is most moving. And what interesting music, deep and full of meaning! And how Mühlfeld plays! As if he had been born for this work. His playing is at once delicate, warm and unaffected and at the same time it shows the most perfect technique and command of the instrument.'[36] Later that month Brahms wrote to her from Vienna that he had long wished for her to hear Mühlfeld, that he knew how sympathetic the man would be to her, and how he would win her heart as an artist. A further important event was the festival organised in May 1894 by the Viennese families Fellinger, Franz and Wittgenstein, of which the highlight was a performance of both the Clarinet Trio and Quintet on 5 May at the Fellingers' home.[37]

Brahms's Clarinet Sonatas Op. 120

In the summer of 1894 Brahms once again retreated to Ischl, where he composed the Sonatas Op. 120 in F minor and in E flat, the keys of Weber's two clarinet concertos. Brahms's intervening opus numbers 116–119 had comprised a series of twenty piano pieces whose predominant characteristic is reflective, introspective and deeply personal, despite occasional energetic outbursts; they are thus in some ways closely related to the clarinet sonatas. Pamela Weston notes that the sonatas were completed by the time Fritz Steinbach and his wife came to stay, in the middle of September. 'On the 19th the three friends travelled to Berchtesgaden, where it had been arranged for the sonatas to be tried over in the presence of the Duke ... Mühlfeld rehearsed the sonatas first with Frau Franz (née Wittgenstein), for the benefit of the composer.'[38] Duke Georg and Baroness von Heldburg came over from Bad Gastein for a private performance at the Berchtesgaden home of Princess Marie, the duke's daughter by his first marriage to Princess Charlotte of Prussia. During November arrangements were made for Clara to hear the sonatas, Brahms writing in advance:

> I have to tell you about something which will cause us both a little annoyance. Mühlfeld will be sending you his tuning fork, so that the grand piano with which he is to play may be tuned to it. His clarinet only allows him to yield very little to other instruments.[39]

It may be assumed that this was to keep the pitch down to his preferred a'=440. The sonatas were played on the 10th and two days later at a party at the family Sommerhoff, together with Mozart's Clarinet

Trio. At a party at Clara's on the 13th were played the sonatas and Schumann's *Phantasiestücke*, and on the 19th there was a further performance at Altenstein Castle (near Schweina) at the invitation of the duke. The first public performance took place on 7 January 1895 at the Tonkünstlerverein in Vienna. Pamela Weston notes further performances on 10 and 11 January, on 27 January (Leipzig) and 17 February (Frankfurt). There were also performances in Rüdesheim and Mannheim prior to a concert in Meiningen on 21 February, at which both the E flat Sonata and the Quintet were played. During subsequent tours that year, Mühlfeld played the sonatas with other pianists, including Julius Röntgen, Fanny Davies and Eugen d'Albert.

Interestingly, Brahms preferred the clarinet and piano medium to that with strings, finding a better blend from the combination.[40] The sound-world of the sonatas is further differentiated by Brahms's choice of the more muscular B♭ clarinet. In a perceptive discussion of both works, Musgrave notes the sheer resourcefulness in the balance and exploitation of the two instruments' distinctive characters.[41] As he remarks, there seems no rein on Brahms's natural expression as a pianist, yet the clarinet is always scored appropriately. For Mac-Donald, 'the works display a kaleidoscopic range of colour and emotion, a propensity for mercurial shifts of texture and harmony – indeed they are prime examples of that "economy, yet richness" which Schoenberg so admired in Brahms'.[42] The opening of the F minor Sonata recalls the mood of the Quintet, though its more economical and smaller-scaled ideas are worked more tautly with a sharing of material characteristic of this later period. The power of expression of the development is compressed into an even smaller space than in the Quintet. The slow movement has a reflective, improvisatory character fusing the rhapsodic aspect of the clarinet idiom with a pianism typical of the late period. By comparison, the E flat Sonata can be regarded as more Classical in its directness of lyrical expression, a fluid first movement containing atmospheric passages of impressionistic quality. Indeed, exploration of colour is an important feature of its ever-developing material. The final variations exploit the reflective and impassioned aspects of the clarinet's personality, concerned with simplification of the asymmetrical theme rather than its elaboration.

The Sonatas' status as the first extended works for clarinet and piano by a major composer since Weber's *Grand Duo Concertant* of 1816 (notwithstanding Schumann's fine character pieces) ensured that they were not eclipsed by the Quintet. Tovey remarked that in any case the Sonatas were from the outset regarded as smaller works. Although all four of Brahms's clarinet works were furnished with alternative parts for viola (another of the composer's favourite instruments), the rescoring of the Trio and Quintet has never proved popular. However, as viola sonatas, Op. 120 achieved lasting success, making a similarly important contribution to an otherwise threadbare repertory.[43] Their suitability for the viola continues to prove a topic for animated discussion amongst clarinettists and others. MacDonald (p. 369) actually expresses a preference for the viola, 'whose darker, huskier tone seems to suit their elusive moods even better than the veiled and silken clarinet'. The validity of this comment with regard to Mühlfeld's Baermann–Ottensteiner clarinets (as opposed to the Boehm system) remains to be proved. Tovey pointed to Brahms's fine demonstration of the different characters of the instruments:

> The viola is querulous and strained just where the cantabile of the clarinet is warmest. The lowest octave of the clarinet is of a dramatic blue-grotto hollowness and coldness, where the fourth string of the viola is of a rich and pungent warmth. A comparison of Brahms's viola part with his original clarinet part makes every difference of this kind vividly real, and these viola versions deserve frequent performances in public.[44]

It is significant that, as Tovey observed, the relation of the clarinet to the string parts in the Trio and Quintet makes it impossible to change the position of anything, and transcription accordingly reveals all the points where the viola fails to represent a clarinet. In addition, the Quintet contains material which lies outside the range of idioms which are truly appropriate to the viola.

Mühlfeld's final decade

During the remainder of Brahms's lifetime, the Quintet continued to exercise a deeply moving effect on its audiences. Among Mühlfeld's tours featuring performances with local quartets was a visit to England

4.1 Richard Mühlfeld with members of the Wendling Quartet, *c.* 1899

in February 1895 when the Quintet was played twice with the violinist Wilma Norman-Neruda.[45] On another occasion Mühlfeld's performance with the Kneisel Quartet rendered the audience speechless, the conductor Nikisch falling to his knees in front of Brahms. In March 1897 Mühlfeld came to Vienna to perform Walther Rabl's Quartet Op. 1 for clarinet, violin, cello and piano, which had won the prize competition organised at Brahms's request by the Tonkünstlerverein 'for the furtherance of wind-instrument music.'[46] A rehearsal at the Wittgensteins' was to have included the Brahms Quintet, but when the by now very sick composer turned up unexpectedly, he requested the Weber Quintet rather than his own. Mühlfeld last met Brahms on 25 March at the house of one Dr Müller and, on returning to Meiningen, received news of the composer's death on 3 April. He travelled back to Vienna for the funeral. Mühlfeld remained in the service of the Duke of Meiningen for the last decade of his life and continued to be fêted and honoured. Figure 4.1 shows him *c.* 1899 with the Wendling Quartet from the Meiningen court orchestra, whose members were Karl Wendling, August Funk, Karl Piening and Alfons Abbass.

43

Mühlfeld inspired a number of other works, including Gustav Jenner's Sonata Op. 5 (1900), Theodor Verhey's Concerto Op. 47 (1901) and Carl Reinecke's *Introduzione ed Allegro appasionata* Op. 256 (1901).[47] Clarinet quintets were composed for him by Stephan Krehl (1902) and Henri Marteau (1909). Pamela Weston has recounted many details of Mühlfeld's final years. He visited England every year between 1899 and 1907 (except for 1903 and 1904), including a notable visit in 1906 with the Joachim Quartet (see Fig. 4.2).[48] Steinbach was succeeded as conductor of the Meiningen orchestra by Wilhelm Berger, who formed an ensemble with Mühlfeld and cellist Karl Piening and wrote a Trio Op. 94 for them.[49] After a visit to Madrid with the Bohemian Quartet in February 1907 Mühlfeld returned to Meiningen, where he unexpectedly died of a cerebral haemorrhage on 1 June.

By way of a postscript it must be noted that an important source for the reception history of Brahms's works during the period 1890–1902 is the Leipzig *Musikalisches Wochenblatt.* Its regular columns 'Concert Report' and 'Performances of New Works' reveal that the fifty verified performances of the Clarinet Quintet during the two years after its composition did not depress the number of performances of the string quartets, but rather occurred in addition to them. In analysing these reports, Kross has noted that in sharp contrast to the Clarinet Quintet the string quintets were rarely performed, the G major being played only twice during the period between 1898 and 1902.[50]

The Brahms Quintet after Mühlfeld

Brahms's early biographers were unanimous in their admiration for the Clarinet Quintet. Florence May's enthusiastic critique of 1905 has already been cited in the preface to this book. H. C. Colles was another immediate captive.[51] Later writers were in total agreement, Tovey describing the Quintet as 'one of the most original and also one of the most pathetic of all Brahms's works'.[52] Mason observed that 'the two essential powers of Brahms's genius, the power to conceive elements of a simplicity that give them universality, and the power to evoke from them an undreamed richness of meaning, reach in the Clarinet Quintet their incomparable perfection.'[53] In *The Musical Times* of 1935 George Dyson attempted in an analysis to explain Brahms's composi-

QUEEN'S HALL

SOLE LESSEES · · · · CHAPPELL & CO. LTD.

JOACHIM COMMITTEE CONCERTS

Spring Season of 1906

LAST CONCERT OF THE SERIES.

Saturday Afternoon, May 12th

At 3

Dr. JOACHIM

THE JOACHIM QUARTET

Prof. RICHARD MÜHLFELD

AND OTHER EMINENT ARTISTS.

TICKETS: Grand Circle and Stalls, 10s. 6d., 7s. 6d., and 5s.; Balcony, 2s. 6d.; Orchestra and Area, 1s.

May be obtained from Messrs. CHAPPELL & Co.'s BOX OFFICE, QUEEN'S HALL, and 50, New Bond Street, W.; the usual Agents; and of

CONCERT DIRECTION E. L. ROBINSON,

7, WIGMORE STREET,

Telephone: 793 Mayfair.
Telegrams: "Musikchor, London."

CAVENDISH SQUARE, W.

PLEASE TURN OVER

4.2 Programme cover for a 1906 London concert, signed by members of the Joachim Quartet for presentation to Richard Mühlfeld

45

tional mastery within the work. The Quintet, together with the Trio and the Sonatas, made an immediate and continuing impact on the clarinet repertory, contributing in no small measure to the instrument's prominent profile throughout the twentieth century. Reger's clarinet works show Brahms's immediate influence, while the repertory for clarinet quintet was enhanced overall, especially in England (see Chapter 7).

The development of recorded sound has enabled different approaches to the Quintet to be effectively compared, a subject which forms an important part of the discussion of performance practice in Chapter 6. 1917 marked the first (partial) recording by Charles Draper, who had heard Mühlfeld in London and whose performances of the Quintet with the Joachim and the Léner Quartets brought him great success. His 1928 recording and that of 1937 by Reginald Kell were important landmarks, but it is since the Second World War that recordings have appeared in quantity, there being at least fifty versions by 1985.[54] MacDonald neatly summarised the Quintet's status a century after its composition: it 'has since remained one of Brahms's most popular works in any medium, for its perfect expression of a spirit of mellow reflection, tinged with autumnal melancholy'.[55]

5

Design and structure

Introduction

Although Brahms's Clarinet Quintet is traditionally regarded as an autumnal and even nostalgic work, its formal architecture is in no sense reactionary. Furthermore, Brahms's integration of clarinet and strings is a substantial achievement in its own right, with fewer opportunities for bravura than for refined musicality, intimate expression and beautiful tone. While the Quintet's nostalgic elements have tended to be emphasised in performance, there are darker and more vigorous aspects to the material, including the fantastic gypsy music in the Adagio. In this part of the work the clarinet moves momentarily to centre stage from its role as *primus inter pares*. The clarinet's large effective range, tonal flexibility and dynamic variety enable it variously to merge with the strings and to stand out clearly as soloist. The richness of the A clarinet emphasises the sombre colours of the instrument's lowest register, as well as providing an extra low semitone not available on the more brilliant B♭.

The character and mood of Brahms's Clarinet Quintet is markedly influenced by the degree to which the tonic key of B minor prevails. Even though the Adagio is in B major, it contains a tinge of minor and has a middle section emphatically within that mode. The third movement begins in D major, but the single definite modulation in the first section is to B minor. Its Presto is a complete sonata movement in B minor, turning to D only at the end. Within the finale there is only one excursion from the tonic for the fifth variation in B major. There can scarcely ever have been a work of such length so bound to one tonality. Another extraordinary feature is that each movement closes at a quiet dynamic. The thematic material of the Quintet is equally characteristic, with a falling motto theme permeating each of the four movements

Ex. 5.1   Falling motif in each of the movements of the Clarinet Quintet

(Ex. 5.1) to produce a cyclic effect.[1] H. C. Colles described this phe-
nomenon as follows: 'Every one of the [Quintet's] principal themes
droops from a high note; so constant is the outline that it is possible to
imagine that all are continuous variants of one idea, and when the
actual melody of the first movement comes back as a coda to the ...
Finale, it hardly seems to be ... a return to an idea long left behind, but
merely the last word on one which has been present to the mind
throughout.'[2] During the course of the Quintet Brahms invests this
simplest of ideas with ever increasing meaning and distinction. Such
economy of method produces a depth of expression which represents
the culmination of a lifetime of experience. A further example of
Brahms's late stylistic simplicity is his willingness in the Quintet to
repeat material literally, not only in the sonata movements 1 and 3, but
within the ternary pattern of the Adagio.

There are some clear parallels with Mozart's Clarinet Quintet, not
least in terms of form. Each work contains an opening sonata movement, a ternary slow movement and a concluding set of variations. In
his finale Mozart's third variation contains melodic contours for the
viola which resemble Brahms's cello variation. Mozart's fourth variation may be regarded as the forerunner of Brahms's third, both featuring semiquaver figuration. Furthermore, Brahms's Quintet follows
Mozart's precedent in assigning the principal material to clarinet and
first violin, at least within his first two movements. As remarked upon
in Chapter 1, each combines a genius for composition with a remarkable gift for instrumental scoring. Both quintets demand technical
expertise and superb control of all aspects of clarinet playing, coupled
with a maturity of interpretative thought. The incidental nature of
Brahms's technical demands is well captured by Homer Ulrich:

It may have been Brahms' purpose here to display the clarinet to advantage. Certainly every opportunity is given to that instrument; lyric melody, dramatic figuration, rhapsodic utterance, delicate passage work, and complete range are employed. But the quintet is in no sense merely a virtuoso display piece; it is an example of perfectly conceived, lovingly planned chamber music of the highest quality.[3]

This comment recalls Maczewski's remark about Brahms's own piano playing in his Brahms article for the first edition of *Grove's Dictionary*: 'Remarkable as his technical execution may be, with him it always seems a secondary casual matter, only to be noticed incidentally'.

Allegro

Although the outlines of Brahms's first movement may readily be understood in terms of traditional sonata form, this music is more usefully regarded as a very subtle example of the sonata principle. Its characteristic ebb and flow of intensity is created by Brahms's fluent treatment of rhythm, texture and dynamics, allied to a sure sense of instrumental colour and an ability continuously to develop his principal material. His freedom and inventiveness within conventional boundaries achieve a formal synthesis which reveals itself only after repeated listening and knowledge of the music. The movement as a whole well illustrates the complex and intricate nature of Brahms's thought processes, a focus of attention for many commentators. Apposite here is Hadow's remark by that 'by his own genius [Brahms] has made the forms wider and more flexible and has shown once more that they are not artificial devices but the organic embodiment of artistic life'. Geiringer observes, 'It is characteristic of him that where he confined himself within the strictest formal bounds his imagination soared to its most magnificent heights'.[4]

Tonal ambiguity is a feature at the outset of the Quintet, the opening two bars giving no indication that the principal tonality will be anything other than D major. There is a clear precedent for this procedure in Haydn's String Quartet Op. 33 no. 1, whose main key only gradually emerges as B minor at the outset. In Brahms's Quintet, the entire four bars preceding the entry of the clarinet are clearly of great significance, comprising the two-bar motif at Example 5.2 which

Ex. 5.2   I/1–3

Ex. 5.3   Original version from I/10

returns at various points later in the Quintet, followed by the related falling motif already illustrated in Example 5.1/I. The entry of the clarinet at bar 5 was described by Heuberger during Brahms's lifetime as 'like some personage duly appointed to lead the body of strings, by apparently testing its strength in each part of its compass and then falling to meditation upon a low F sharp'.[5] It is undoubtedly true that bars 5–13 offer an eloquent introduction to the character of the clarinet, the initial entry at bar 5 highlighted as the only articulated voice on the main beat. Incidentally, it is remarkable to observe from Brahms's manuscript that bars 10ff were originally contoured as in Example 5.3 and only at the eleventh hour altered in a way which incomparably heightens the effect of the passage.[6]

Although this sonata movement is generally orthodox, its first subject has divided analytical opinion. Evans chose to regard the first thirteen bars of the movement as a preamble to the first subject proper. More responsive to the music itself is Pascall's analysis of the first subject as a four–bar statement containing two thematic notions which are afterwards expanded in order within the twenty-bar response which follows.[7] Thus bars 5–13 present an elaboration of bars 1–2, with bars 14–24 developing bars 3–4. Bar 5 represents a horizontal unfolding of the D major implied in bar 1, while the clarinet's bars 8–9 relate to 6–7 in the same way that the violins' bar 2 relates to bar 1; bars 10–13 continue to elaborate existing material, bar 13 containing a clear reference to the opening bar. Diminution of the clarinet's opening arpeggio plays a significant role within the string accompaniment. At bar 14 intensity of sonority is achieved by the placement of the cello above the viola, recalling a similar colour in the second subject of Brahms's Second Symphony. The first tonic chord of B minor occurs only at bar 18, where thematic continuation incorporates an ingenious arpeggio-derived counterpoint in clarinet and viola (bars 18–22) culminating in a characteristic hemiola at bar 24, where the approach to the cadence elaborates bar 17. Thus in the first twenty-four bars there already is an enormous concentration of material.

The transition (bars 24–36) acts as far more than a bridge passage, since it provides an important contrast of character with both main themes, whilst at the same time modulating to the relative major. Bar 25 introduces a new rhythmically dramatic element and remarkably the following bars relate closely to both subjects, circling in bars 26 and 27 around the notes from bar 1, while introducing quaver movement with anacrusis (albeit staccato) which will feature within the second subject (Ex. 5.4a). The effect here is to shift forward the strings a quaver in advance of the beat until the clarinet intervenes to restore the conventional accent. As Evans observes, 'a more ingenious and at the same time artistic manner of giving prominence to this instrument could certainly not be devised'.[8]

The second subject in D from bar 36 continues the syncopation over a dominant pedal, its stepwise movement forming a clear link with bar 1. Thematic material is distributed among the ensemble, with felicitous scoring and octave doublings. New derivatives arise, including Example 5.4b, first heard in bars 41–2 in second violin and viola and taken up immediately in first violin and clarinet. D major cadences are conspicuously avoided; indeed the music diverts to C major for four bars at bar 47. The continuation at bar 48 is different in treatment rather than material; subdued in character and low in tessitura, it allows the clarinet entry at bar 51 to make a special effect, whilst the

Ex. 5.4a I/25–7, violin 1

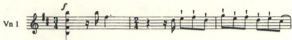

Ex. 5.4b I/41–2, violin 2

chromatic nature of the material produces some colourful harmonies. At the approach to the imperfect cadence in D at bar 58 comes a direct reference in bar 56 to Example 5.4b.

The following passage from bar 58 may usefully be regarded as a codetta, though it remains related to previous material. With each anacrusis accented, it combines the rhythmic impetus of the second subject with the accented dissonance of bar 3, adding a leggiero triplet figure in bar 62 at the start of a four-bar string passage which heralds a final delicate clarinet entry at bar 66. In the last two bars the initial 'circling' motif is adroitly introduced and for the repeat of the exposition this replaces the opening four bars. The repeat of the exposition is thus neatly disguised, with bars 3 and 4 completely absent yet with the flow of the music intact.

The development occurs at greater length than is usual for Brahms, occupying a total of sixty-five bars (71–135). Its opening (bars 71–80) acts as an introduction, its static quality serving to disguise the beginning of the thematic working out. Based on the principal circling motif from bars 1–2 and the clarinet arpeggio from bar 5, this passage effects a leisurely modulation from D major to C♯ minor, darkened not only by the harmonic vocabulary but by the colour of the lowest notes of the clarinet's chalumeau register. As the crescendo begins at bar 81 there is a sense of new beginning, heralding the start of an intense treatment of the circling motif which continues until bar 97. The counterpoint in the clarinet at bar 81 heard subsequently in the strings can be traced to elements of the accompaniment in bars 6–10. An imperfect cadence at bar 87 leads to further rhythmic interest as a three–note figure derived from the first three notes of the circling motif is earnestly combined with the whole motif itself. The occurrence of inversion, sequence and stretto gives this passage a slightly academic turn not unlike the analogous area of Mozart's Clarinet Quintet. It is in fact all the more effective for its contrast with the predominantly lyrical exposition. The manner in which the three-note figure migrates to various parts of the bar is sufficient to elevate the music above Evans's dismissive assessment of this passage as 'mere workmanship'.

The transition material from bars 25ff forms the basis for bars 98–120. The marking of *piano quasi sostenuto* at bar 98 indicates that the previously dramatic material has been given an altogether gentler focus, as the music modulates enharmonically to D flat. The sonority of the clarinet's lowest note (sounding *d♭*) colours this important bar, which introduces a passage of glowing cantabile. The rhythm of bar 98 remains a feature of the accompaniment for the whole passage, whose main element is a transformation of bars 26 and 27 into material of exquisite lyricism. A shift to A major at bar 106 has the clarinet playing for the first time the motif from bars 25 and 98, prior to a dialogue with the first violin. The climax of this passage (bar 114) slips briefly into C major, after which the various motifs combine as the music subsides dynamically, while passing through C minor, D major and minor, B flat major and minor before moving enharmonically at bar 121 to the dominant of B minor. The final part of the development (or retransition) from bar 121 begins with further reference to bar 26 together with its inversion, a prominent dominant pedal in the cello and effective displacement of the pulse. This throws into relief a highly idiomatic reference in the clarinet (bars 127–8) to the second element of the first subject (bars 3–4). A chromatic working of the circling motif in clarinet and cello within and under a dominant pedal (bars 131–5) leads to the recapitulation at a level of inspiration worthy of Mozart.

The arrival of the recapitulation is instantly recognisable from bars 136–7, which however lead immediately to a rescoring of bars 14ff. Neither the harmonic ambiguity nor the wide-ranging clarinet utterance of bars 5ff needs to be recalled at this stage in the movement. The transition is also contracted and now modulates (with less prominence for the clarinet) to G major for the second subject at bar 157. Bars 36 to 66 undergo felicitous rescoring as bars 157 to 187, during which it becomes clear that for Brahms the upper limit of clarinet writing in lyrical music is no higher than eb''' or e'''. The downward shift from D to C major at bar 48 finds a parallel in the move from G to F at bar 169, the melody now scored at once for the clarinet.

The continuity of Brahms's music here has divided analytical opinion as to the start of the coda. The final four bars (67–70) of the exposition are not recalled but are replaced at bars 188ff by a thematically related but agitated passage of orchestral intensity, characterised by measured string tremolos. At the climax of this (bars 195–6) the circling motif of bars 1 and 2 is fully harmonised with seventh chords, followed by two bars of downward clarinet roulades (inverting bar 28) and the subject from bar 3 in the first violin over a tonic pedal of b. As the music subsides (bars 199–205), there are references to many preceding elements, including the decoration of the circling motif previously heard in the approach to the recapitulation, the second element of the first subject from bars 3–4, together with tremolo and syncopated accompaniment figures. A B minor melodic arpeggio through the strings leads in bars 207–10 to a final reminiscence of bars 1–4 (minus syncopation in viola and cello), leaving the clarinet to lead a final eight bars of subdued resignation. The transference of the half-bar dissonance in bars 3 and 4 to the main beat of bars 212 and 214 adds an extra poignancy, as does the scoring of the very end, where a solo clarinet cadence is followed by two quietly sober tonic chords, where the clarinet takes the fifth, sounding $f\sharp$.

Adagio

The slow movement presents the two extremes of simplicity of outline and elaboration of detail. Thematic transformation continues throughout the tripartite form, as can be seen from a comparison of bar 1 with the opening of the central section at bar 52 (IIa and IIb in Ex. 5.1). Yet in character these two main elements in the movement could not be more contrasted. The texture of the opening eight bars is richly imaginative, with the initial four bars of clarinet melody freely imitated by the violin at the distance of one-and-a-half beats. As in the Larghetto of Mozart's Clarinet Quintet, the strings are muted throughout. The theme itself immediately calls to mind the opening of

Ex. 5.5   II/17–21, violin 1

the second movement of Brahms's own F major String Quintet. The
triplet and duple elements in the lower three voices diminish the
feeling of regular pulse and contribute to a homogeneous rhythmic
flow which is very unusual within the medium of chamber music. The
seven bars of clarinet melody are extended to eight by means of an
overlapping rescoring of bars 5–6, with the melody transferred to the
second violin.[9] The opening of the movement offers immediate harmonic interest, the first violin colouring the very first bar of B major
with the flattened sixth, which forms the basis of the chord of the
seventh at the climax in bar 5. A rescoring of the opening phrase forms
bars 9–16, in which clarinet and first violin exchange roles, with some
rhythmic changes of detail in the lower parts. Brahms has orchestrated
this passage in such a way that the triplet figuration is completed only
by the violin melody itself. At bar 16 the clarinet transforms bar 8 so as
to lead into a reflective melodic line deriving from bar 5. Starting at
bar 17 an octave countermelody in the violins takes bar 7 as its starting
point (Ex. 5.5), this entire contrasting section culminating in striking
downward leaps in the clarinet in bar 24, prefacing an arpeggiated solo
passage in bars 25–6. The transition back to the main theme (bars 27–
31) is based on its first three notes, expanded to four in a manner
which momentarily suspends the feeling of pulse. The exquisite tonal
digression here has Neapolitan chords falling to seventh chords in C
sharp minor (bar 28) and B minor (bar 30), returning to the opening
material via a German sixth in bar 31. A highly effective rescoring of
bars 1–4 leads now to a Neapolitan *sf* chord at bar 36, after which the
strings continue with a subdued reworking of bars 5–8, incorporating
a delicious contrast of sharpened- and flattened-sixth and seventh
degrees of the scale in the violin melody. A final shift from major to
minor (bar 41) prepares for the entry of the clarinet and its ten-bar link
passage which serves to introduce the drama of the middle section.

No modulation is effected between bars 41 and the start of the *più
lento* at bar 52, and it seems that this intervening recitative-like passage

is intended as preparation for the contrasting music which follows. At an evocative *piano* dynamic the clarinet moves to the forefront of the ensemble with solo flourishes which patently derive from the circling motif at the beginning of the first movement, whilst at the same time offering a foretaste of the oncoming mood. During the subsidence of the climax at bar 46, the triplets, which have already played a major part in accompaniment figuration during the movement, are introduced into the clarinet part. Meanwhile, the strings have constant references to the opening bar of the Adagio, finally quoting it verbatim (with fermata) at bar 51.

As we noted in the Preface, the *più lento* (bars 52–86) has long been recognised for its striking originality. Here Brahms allows himself to use the virtuoso capacity of the clarinet, turning the quartet into a miniature orchestra employing tremolo, rich double-stopping and elaborate decoration. A high emotional voltage is achieved by means of relatively simple harmonic language. It has been argued that the whole passage reflects Brahms's experience of Hungarian gypsy bands, in which the clarinet might sometimes take role of leader. But the virtuosity here is always tasteful and characteristically coherent in terms of form. Indeed, the improvisatory quality of Brahms's music invites comparison with the wild Hungarian lament written by Haydn a hundred years earlier in the second movement of his C major Quartet Op. 54 no. 2, where the first violin breaks into impassioned arabesques above a dark and brooding melody.

Brahms begins with three elaborate embellishments (bars 52ff, 58ff and 64ff) of the first bar of the principal subject, with the metre changed to 4/4; these gradually increase in intensity as the movement proceeds. The clarinet virtuosity incorporates fluency in fast scales and arpeggios in each opening pairs of bars, which are followed by a cadential melody in longer note values related in contour to bars 27–31. In bars 52–6 the accompaniment is relatively simple, though with some anticipation of the clarinet line at the beginning of bar 54 and the introduction of tremolo in first violin and viola. The interlude of bars 56–7 comprises a simple rumination in the strings on the frenzy of what has just taken place, built around the note $f\sharp'$ in the first violin; amongst the F sharp minor and B minor harmonies a subsidiary melodic line in the second violin has an augmented version of the previous half

Ex. 5.6 II/69–70

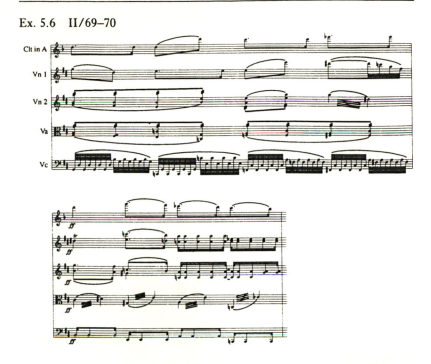

bar in the clarinet. A rising scale in the clarinet acts as an anacrusis to a restatement in bars 58–63 of bars 52–7, though a substantial increase in intensity is achieved by a more generous use of tremolo in all the string parts, extending into the interlude in bars 62–3. The passage from bar 64 comprises a radical, more florid reinterpretation of what has gone before: the clarinet tessitura is higher and more wide ranging, whilst the harmonies are less stable, passing in bars 64–5 through A major and minor and G major. The material is extended in bars 68–71 by the development of a syncopated figure from the accompaniment of the previous bar. The approach to the climax at bar 70 features dialogue between clarinet and first violin and frenzied lower parts, notably the cello (Ex. 5.6). The culmination of this is achieved through the high tessitura of the clarinet part and simultaneous syncopation in different note values. The ruminative string postlude in bars 72–3 is now based around the note *b'*, with tremolo confined to the cello.

An element of fantasy in bars 74–86 comprises a further development of material and transition to the principal theme of the move-

Ex. 5.7 II/74–8, clarinet and violin I

ment. Firstly, there is a return to triple metre, whilst string references to bar 5 are answered by two ever more ornate clarinet flourishes (bars 75, 77), whose third beats consist of the dotted rhythm which has played such a major part in the middle section (Ex. 5.7). The underlying crescendo is intensified by the strings in bar 78, leading to the second component of this passage at bars 79–84. The dotted rhythm now forms the basis of a climactic display of the clarinet's upper and lower registers, including wide-ranging leaps reminiscent of Mozart's idioms. Tremolo returns to the strings whilst in bars 79 and 80 the cello has an augmented version of the clarinet's theme from bars 52ff. Thirdly, there are two 4/4 bars (85–6) of free-wheeling elaboration of the gypsy music, which are the most technically challenging for the clarinet in the whole piece. This passionate outburst is linked to the recapitulation via bar 87 in the most imaginative and adroit manner. The preceding chord of E flat minor in bar 86 becomes enharmonically D sharp, i. e. the mediant chord in B major, which resolves on to a dominant seventh on the half bar. Meanwhile, the first violin has the principal theme extended by one beat, above rising arpeggios derived from the middle section in cello, viola and (as an anacrusis to the return of the main theme) the clarinet. Since the violin ended with the pitches of bar 1 in bar 87, the recapitulation begins from the equivalent of bar 2; from bar 88 to 127 the material is repeated, with only a modification of the final chord in preparation for the coda.

Over a *pianissimo* seventh chord in bar 128 the clarinet recalls its decorative phrases from the middle section, though more slowly and lyrically, and in the major mode. An echo from the first violin sinks on to the final chord, through which the clarinet climbs by delicate arpeggios to a last falling third. One feels compelled to agree wholeheartedly that 'it is at once one of the simplest and one of the most beautiful endings in all chamber music'.[10]

Andantino – Presto non assai, ma con sentimento

At least one writer has suggested that there is a decline in the level of inspiration in the final two movements of the Clarinet Quintet.[11] Evans regarded the third movement as 'so decidedly inferior to Brahms's best work that its good points run the risk of being underrated'. But the sheer inventiveness of the third movement at once makes this a difficult argument to sustain. As has often been observed, Brahms was at the same time too serious and too fastidious for the scherzo of his predecessors, and comedy did not come naturally to him. He was therefore obliged to invent a new type of scherzo or a substitute for it, presenting three distinctive solutions in his first three symphonies and yet another in the Clarinet Quintet. The esoteric Andantino–Presto movement here constitutes what Pascall describes as a frame;[12] the scherzo is the 2/4 Presto, whereas the 4/4 introduction acts as a quasi-trio element and is also a generative section for most of the ensuing sonata movement. The Andantino material returns only in the final nine bars of the movement, but notated as if part of the Presto section. Throughout the movement Brahms is sparing with his motifs but proves his ability to change their character in some quite remarkable ways.

The character of the D major Andantino forms a perfect bridge from the mood of the Adagio to the scherzo proper, whilst concealing the broad emotional span that has been traversed. Its form, which can be tabulated as AABA, resembles that of the opening part of the Adagio. The opening strain in the clarinet is seven bars in length, with an accompaniment in viola and cello; the predominantly contrary motion of the bass line to the tune gives some impression of counterpoint where virtually none exists. As so often, the repeat of the melody involves the violin an octave higher than the clarinet; there are some modest changes in the lower parts and an extension in bar 13 to make a conventional eight-bar phrase. The middle section (bars 16–28) begins

Ex. 5.8a   III/19–21, violin 2

Ex. 5.8b   III/34–5

as if to elaborate the main theme, introducing arpeggiated accompaniment in the cello. A new motif at the *forte* climax in bar 19 (Ex. 5.8a)
appears at this stage incidental, but will assume considerable importance later in the movement. Like many themes in the Quintet it is the
subject of thematic transfer between violin and clarinet, and it can also
be seen to derive quite obviously from bars 41–2 (Ex. 5.4b) in the first
movement. Subsequently, a series of broken arpeggios (bars 23–8)
shared between viola, first violin and clarinet over a tonic pedal leads
to the return of the main theme. Reduced to five bars, this return
begins with material in the clarinet from bars 1 and 3, whilst in the
violins a pedal is decorated with references to the first two beats of the
clarinet's initial melody.

The scherzo (bars 34ff) comprises a miniature sonata movement,
closely related thematically to the Andantino.[13] This relationship is
immediately explicit, the main Presto theme being an obvious transformation of the first bar of the movement; it provides an excellent
example of Brahms's ability to alter the character of material almost
(but not quite) beyond recognition. Rhythmically it comprises two
elements, of which the dotted rhythm of the second beat can be recalled during the movement without recourse to its neutral melodic
contour (Ex. 5.8b) Meanwhile, the accompaniment in the second violin and viola relates directly to the important figure (Ex. 5.8a) at bar 19

of the Andantino. The dynamic marking *molto p mezza voce* contributes to the whole effect. The semiquavers of the first beat undergo some development as early as the fifth bar (bar 38), while the dotted rhythm of the second is quickly expanded. The idiomatic downward flourish (bar 43) which is the clarinet's first entry is an arresting touch, which can be related thematically to the arpeggios within the Andantino. This gesture and its inversion infect the transition to the dominant minor in bars 44–53, at the end of which passage come some overt inversions of the opening Presto bar. The contour of the syncopated second subject in bar 54 is again derived from Example 5.8a, though so transformed as to give the effect of new material. A restatement at bar 64 has triplet syncopation in the first violin over a pedal in the chalumeau register of the clarinet, which afterwards extends the melody by two bars. The second subject achieves contrast with the earlier music by means of its rhythm and also by the liberal use of pizzicato in the accompaniment.

The development (bars 76–121) begins with an effective rescoring of the main Presto subject, whose reharmonisation points the ambiguity between B minor and D major. A cadential extension at bars 89–91 has an especially effective reinterpretation of the material in triplets. The accompaniment figure has already featured at bar 80 and now becomes the focus of intense attention (bars 92–101) during a *forte* passage based in G major and permeated by the flourish from bar 43. From bar 102 a final disintegration of the main Presto subject occurs, the semiquaver element providing an ostinato, whilst the dotted element assumes a melodic sweep in thirds and sixths throughout the ensemble. The music passes briefly through G minor and D minor before returning to B minor. A related melodic germ at bars 114–17 features an expressive dominant-ninth chord in the dominant F sharp minor. The semiquaver ostinato then transforms into triplets in bars 118–21, whose tension is released only by the return of the main theme.

The recapitulation (bars 122–61) includes some felicitous rescorings in its later stages. The second subject in the tonic (bars 140ff) now has the first violin at the octave and is approached via a Neapolitan chord at bars 136–8. The coda begins at bar 162 in G major and at first recalls the development. The arpeggios from bars 23–8 of the

Andantino reappear. Transformations and fragments of various elements of the first subject in bars 174–7 are underpinned by a D major pedal. The re-entry of the arpeggios in the last of these bars brings at bar 178 a recapitulation not only of the final restatement of the main Andantino theme from bar 29, but also of the three bars which originally preceded it. These are now notated in the 2/4 time-signature of the Presto, giving an essential indication of the relationship between the two tempi, whose crotchet pulse can remain constant throughout the movement. Brahms's restatement of so small a part of the Andantino is a daring step, but one which nevertheless manages to bring a sense of fulfilment to the movement's close.

Con moto

For the finale of the Clarinet Quintet Brahms favours a rigorous pattern of theme, five variations and coda, as in the slow movements of the Sextets Opp. 18 and 36, the Andante con moto of the C major Piano Trio Op. 87 and the finale of the Clarinet Sonata Op. 120 no. 2.[14] Apart from some relaxation at the fourth variation in the major mode, there is a gradual increase in animation which is reversed only at the coda. But the theme remains an overriding influence, so that there is no parallel with Beethoven's 'Diabelli' or Brahms's own 'Handel' sets, where the melody is no more than a starting point for original ideas and moods. Indeed, these variations in the Quintet are of a more traditional, decorative type, recalling Mozart or early Beethoven. The movement's substance derives from the individuality of the variations within a unified whole and from the gradually pervading influence of the first movement, especially within the coda. Whereas in the three earlier movements Brahms creates interest partially through modifications of traditional forms, the interest here is created by ingenious handling of musical materials within a familiar framework.

The formal plan of the theme is AA' //:BA² ://, where both A and B each consist of eight bars. The falling four-note figure which is the principal motif often continues with a rising third, the whole effect (with prominent diminished fourth) recalling the subject matter at bar 14 of the first movement. The texture is entirely homophonic, though

Ex. 5.9   IV/65–7, clarinet and violin 1

with some judicious rhythmical and melodic touches in the inner
parts. The clarinet simply echoes phrase endings until it assumes
the melody in the final eight bars. Just before the central double bar
the harmony turns to D for the cadence before continuing in G
major, the main motif altered melodically but remaining recognisable
in terms of rhythm. The music returns to B minor for the clarinet's
entry at bar 25.

Variation 1 illustrates Brahms's freedom of texture, taking the form
of a wide-ranging cello solo, formulated from the bass line of the
theme but also containing elements of the melody. The wide leaps and
string crossings which outline the chordal structure have been happily
compared by at least one writer with idioms in Bach's solo cello
suites.[15] In the first half of the variation the echo effects are fully
harmonised by the whole ensemble, including a prominent clarinet. In
the second half the texture is denser, introducing imitative points and
a greater degree of chromaticism, whilst its continuous quaver movement prevents too close an association with the theme.

Variation 2 is based on an important variant of the main motif,
related rhythmically, but featuring the interval of a semitone (Ex.
5.9).[16] Though furthest in distance from the theme, this intense variation contains some important reminiscences of earlier movements. For
example, continuous syncopation in the accompaniment recalls bar 3
of the opening movement, while the dotted figure introduced in bar 69
is related to the second beat of the Presto non assai. In this variation
harmonies are more dissonant, the second and fourth bars (66 and 68)
becoming diminished sevenths and bar 76 containing an especially
expressive ninth. Ascending and descending arpeggios throughout the
ensemble recall the passage from bar 43 in the Presto. The second half
begins in contrasting vein, with an eloquent clarinet line developing a
melodic contour whose origins lie within the accompaniment at bars

Ex. 5.10   IV/129–30

69 and 77. The syncopation at this point is smoother and more subdued. Only in the final four bars is there a hint of the main motif in
rhythmic mutation.

Variation 3 develops a motif which combines elements of the circling motif from the first movement with the theme of the finale. In
the first half the violin solo is echoed by the clarinet, an effect deriving
from the original theme. The middle G major section is taken over by
the clarinet in semi-staccato arpeggios, prompting one writer to style
this the 'music-box' variation.[17] The return to B minor (bars 121–8)
contrives some delicious dialogue between the two soloists.

Variation 4 in B major revives a number of previous ideas, whilst
at the same time indicating the outlines of the theme itself.[18] The
opening bars (Ex. 5.10) refer to the semitone motif from variation 2
and the main subject from the Adagio, whilst containing references in
the inner parts to the first movement's circling motif, continuing
the semiquaver motion of the previous variation. Indeed, quaver and
semiquaver motion is a feature of the entire variation, with dialogue
between clarinet and first violin again of primary importance. The
change of mode affects the harmonies of the middle section, which
passes through G sharp minor at bar 148. This passage develops a
motif from bar 133 into an expressive melody which combines effectively with the semitone motif and a momentary return to syncopation
in the inner parts.

Variation 5 reverts to the minor mode but is distinguished by a new

Ex. 5.11   IV/161–6

triple 3/8 metre (Ex. 5.11). The contour of the finale theme can be easily discerned throughout the viola solo, but the wide-ranging pizzicato cello part simultaneously recalls the first variation. Decoration in the clarinet (later together with first violin) comprises diminution of the viola line, whilst contriving to recall the circling motif of the first movement. The middle section recalls bars 3–4 and 14ff of the first movement during a crescendo to the restatement at bar 185, in which the clarinet semiquavers from bars 163–4 assume a pervasive role.

The masterly coda at bar 193 is introduced by a rare *fp*. Hereafter there is no new material, but simply an interaction between motifs from first movement and finale. References to the first movement have been prepared throughout the variations, so that the coda appears as a natural consequence of what has gone before, rather than in any sense an interpolation. To begin with, bars 1–4 of the first movement are at last literally recalled in E minor, cadencing in G (bars 193–6). An extension to the phrase in *pp* octaves (bars 197–9) leads to a reference to the viola theme from the preceding variation (bar 200) and a reinterpretation of the whole passage led by the clarinet (bars 201– 6), this time via C major. As the 'viola' theme is restated in bars 207–10, tonic chords are conspicuously avoided; in bar 210 a final measured cadenza rises in the clarinet and then falls, to present in bars 214–22 a thinly disguised and partly augmented version of the end of the first movement, retaining its essentially low dynamic, except for a richly scored penultimate *forte* chord. As this work of towering intellectual and emotional strength reaches its final conclusion, the effect is almost unbearably poignant.

6

Performance practice

Introduction: the issues

Is the kind of performance expected by Brahms in his own day valid for later generations of players? We can never really answer that question, if only because so many relevant parameters have changed during the last century or so. For example, the discipline imposed by the microphone and the implications of air travel are two factors which have brought about such changes that we cannot turn back the clock. Even if we could hear Richard Mühlfeld's première of Brahms's Quintet we should not necessarily want to adopt all its features; like all performers of our own day we should continue to exercise elements of choice and taste as much characteristic of our own day as Mühlfeld's. But the mere fact that the original performance conditions can now seem at all relevant marks a radical shift in our musical thinking. As this book is being written, players of various nationalities are beginning to think it worthwhile to acquire copies of the Baermann-Ottensteiner clarinets used by Mühlfeld, in an attempt to come closer to his sound-world. Nevertheless, notation in Brahms's scores leaves a number of ambiguities, even though it dates from a period relatively close to our own.

Changes in musical taste

Any assessment of the available documentary and critical evidence needs to take into account the nature of musical taste of the 1890s. Early recordings are an important guide, and the evidence they provide has recently been subject to detailed analysis. Robert Philip, in *Early Recordings and Musical Style* (Cambridge, 1992), has drawn attention to the more spontaneous approach to performance which was the norm before 1900. Since that time, there has been 'a trend towards greater power, firmness, clarity, control, literalness, and evenness of expression, and away from informality, looseness, and unpredictability'.[1] Most recorded performances from the earlier twentieth century give a vivid sense of being projected as if to an audience, the precision and clarity of each note less important than the shape and progress of the music as a whole. Nowadays the balance has shifted significantly, so that accurate and clear performance of the music has become the first priority and the characterisation is assumed to take care of itself. If pre-war recordings resemble live performance, many of today's concerts show a palpable influence of the recording session, with clarity and control an overriding priority.

Today's literal interpretation of note values, whilst allowing some flexibility, makes many early recordings seem almost casual in approach: 'The performances of the early twentieth century ... are volatile, energetic, flexible, vigorously projected in broad outline but rhythmically informal in detail. Modern performances are, by comparison, accurate, restrained, deliberate, and even in emphasis.'[2] As Jon Finson has written,

> The twentieth-century performer seeks the authentic note text, attended by the belief that it is to be faithfully rendered with as few arbitrary additions as possible to sully the composer's intention ... The performer's ability to play the 'notes' accurately and completely is prized above almost all other virtues. And so, having dispensed with the slovenly traditions that marked performances around the turn of the century, the continuous history of playing nineteenth-century music becomes one of steady improvement in technical standards and fidelity to the printed text.[3]

But in point of fact, notation is a shorthand for the entire practice of pitch relationships, durations, ornamentation and timbre. A composer's score has meaning only in the context of its period and this can help to define the bounds of what can be historically determined.

The recorded history of the clarinet broadly reflects the trends observed by Finson, and suggests that most modern performances of the Quintet are some way distant from Mühlfeld's.[4] As far as is known, Mühlfeld himself committed nothing to disc, though technologically this would have been a possibility. There remain various accounts of his playing, useful evidence which nevertheless bears witness to the limitations of words in accurately describing musical interpretation. Descriptions of the playing of both Brahms and Joachim offer supplementary information about general musical principles, and further evidence is contained in Joachim's *Violinschule*.[5] Both these musicians also left a tiny amount of recorded evidence.

Mühlfeld's clarinet playing

The minimal amount of surviving evidence relating to Mühlfeld's personality offers few clues as to his musical character. Members of the family reported that Richard was given neither to criticising nor complaining and never lost his temper.[6] After his death the local Meiningen newspaper simply remarked that he was loved and respected by all who knew him, his generosity as a musician reflected in his personality. His cheerful sincerity bore witness to the character of a human being at peace with himself. Clearly this was an exceptional man, whose execution on the clarinet belied his calm exterior.

Among many individual qualities in his playing, it seems that Mühlfeld's powerful delivery incorporated the liberal use of vibrato.[7] Some evidence for this is offered in a reminiscence recounted by Jack Brymer:

> Just before World War II a question was put to a very old viola-player, sometime conductor of the Duke of Devonshire's Orchestra, about the playing of Mühlfeld. The old man had occasionally been called in by Joachim to play in his quartet, and on several occasions had played the Brahms Quintet with the great Mühlfeld. Of the clarinettist's playing he was most enthusiastic, saying that three things mainly stuck in his memory. 'He used two clarinets, A and B flat, for the slow movement, to simplify the gypsy section; he had a fiery technique with a warm tone – and a big vibrato.' Asked again by a startled questioner if he didn't mean to say '*rubato*' the old man looked puzzled. 'No', he said, 'vibrato – much more than Joachim, and as much as the cellist.' (It will be recalled that Joachim was reputed to play with little or no vibrato.) This account, while of no authority, does at least give one food for thought...[8]

Of course, Mühlfeld's background as a violinist makes his use of vibrato all the more plausible and (for that time) individual and un-usual.

Although vibrato on stringed instruments continued to be regarded as ornamental throughout the nineteenth century, in wind playing it remained controversial. In 1863 it was dismissed by Moritz Haupt-mann, who claimed that a wind note with vibrato was as impossible as a vibrated harmonic.[9] This opinion was contradicted by Arrey von Dommer in 1865, who reckoned that vibrato was effective on both the flute and the oboe.[10] That the technique was becoming more wide-spread is suggested by the instruction at the heading of the intermezzo of Carl Reinecke's 'Undine' Flute Sonata Op. 167, that it should be played 'without any vibrato at all'. Perhaps Mühlfeld was as progres-sive as Joachim was conservative in this respect. As late as 1954 a cautious approach to the subject may be observed in Rendall's book on the clarinet.

Accounts of Mühlfeld's playing emphasise both his musicianship and his tone-quality. There is considerable evidence that Mühlfeld's tone (as well as his delivery) differed markedly from the British tradi-tion. In 1988 Paul Vaughan recalled that his own teacher George Garside (himself renowned for a full, rich, golden sound) once told him that he had been taken as a boy to hear Mühlfeld play the Brahms Quintet; he was a fine technician, 'but his tone was comic'.[11] This may have been a reaction to the employment of heavy vibrato, as well as an emphatic delivery; in addition, the difference in German and English clarinet designs (as well as Mühlfeld's retention of boxwood instru-ments) undoubtedly contributed to the stylistic equation. It has been suggested that anyone from the British clarinet tradition of Henry Lazarus (1815–95), Julian Egerton (1848–1945), Charles Draper (1869–1952) and Frederick Thurston (1901–53) would have found Mühlfeld's tone very 'strong'.[12] This supposition is confirmed in a paper delivered in 1916 by Oscar Street:

> As for Mühlfeld himself, he was undoubtedly a very fine artist; his phrasing was carried to a high pitch of perfection, but his tone and execution at times left much to be desired. The somewhat extravagant praise that was lavished upon him when he visited this country was, I think, in some measure due to the extraordinary national habit of glori-fying foreigners at the expense of our own people, a habit which this

terrible war is doing much to destroy. We have had, and still have, players in some respects his equal, and in others clearly his superior. To mention only the latest performance of the quintet which it was my good fortune to hear – I mean that by one of our leading clarinettists and the London String Quartet only a few weeks ago – nothing could have exceeded the beauty of tone, the perfection of phrasing, and the ensemble to which we were then treated. But at the same time we do not forget that it was due to Richard Mühlfeld's playing that Brahms left us these lovely works, and we honour his memory accordingly.[13]

This was essentially the view of Rendall in 1942, who attributed the 'mild furore' caused in England by Mühlfeld as attributable to the freshness and originality of Brahms's music, the interpretative ability and musicianship of the clarinettist, and the preference for a foreigner, 'which, formerly confined to foreign singers, had during the last fifty years extended itself to instrumentalists as well.' Rendall noted that Mühlfeld played on 'the clumsy Baermann system, which fortunately inspired no following'.[14] This may have been the case in England, but scarcely held true for either Germany or Central Europe.

It was reported in 1971 that 'British musicians alive today who heard both Mühlfeld and Draper play are unanimous in declaring the latter the finer of the two. The late Vaughan Williams was of this opinion also, and felt that where Mühlfeld played with the tone and fire of a violinist ... Draper brought out the true quality of the clarinet.'[15] Similarly, George Bernard Shaw found the sound rich, but not so pure as that of Lazarus, England's foremost player at the time of Mühlfeld's first visits. There is more to these criticisms than mere British chauvinism. Mühlfeld was clearly a highly individual player and thus likely to divide musical opinion even on his own territory. Friedrich Buxbaum, who had been cellist in the Rosé Quartet and had played the Trio with Mühlfeld during Brahms's lifetime, commented in 1940 that there were plenty of better clarinettists in Vienna in the 1890s.[16] Anthony Baines wrote in 1957 that 'Mühlfeld ... is remembered in Vienna as having been admired more for technique than for his tone, which was heavy and over-predominating'.[17] In 1954 Rendall continued to be ambivalent: 'technically he was no doubt inferior to some of his contemporaries. Opinions of his tone and intonation vary. Some competent critics found him deficient in both; others praised the velvety quality of his lower register.'[18] But Rendall did concede that, after Mühlfeld, the clarinet was looked upon not merely as an orchestral instrument but as an instrument capable of the highest range of expression in solo and chamber music.[19]

Whatever the judgement of posterity, there were certainly a number of eminent contemporaries besides Brahms who were captivated by Mühlfeld's talent. Liszt (who probably heard him at Bayreuth) compared his tone to the sensation of biting into a ripe peach.[20] As we have noted, another celebrated admirer was Richard Wagner. Clara Schumann's response to Mühlfeld's playing, already cited on pages 39–40, is especially informative and evocative, both in relation to his artistry and craftsmanship. The depth and richness of his tone were doubtless assisted by the mellower A clarinet for which the Trio and Quintet are scored, and also his adherence to a low pitch at a time when it was tending to rise.

The viola player cited by Brymer raised an interesting technical point – Mühlfeld's use of the B flat clarinet during the central part of the slow movement. The matter was again raised in correspondence during 1989, Paul Vaughan believing that he had heard the same story from George Garside.[21] At least one early edition has the six bars (only) before the reprise of the main theme and the initial six-bar strain of the recapitulation transposed for B flat, as Jonathan Rutland subsequently illustrated.[22] As a result, a pair of particularly awkward (and notorious) arpeggios notated in F sharp minor can be played in the much more grateful key of F minor.

The string quartet

Modifications to the sound of the string quartet since Brahms's time have arisen partly from the material of the strings themselves: whereas steel wire is frequently used for the uppermost string on the violin and the upper strings of the cello today, such strings were not generally used during the latter part of the nineteenth century. Instead, both instruments were strung with unwound gut on the upper two strings and wound gut (also common today) on the bottom strings. As late as 1924 Carl Flesch wrote that while steel is more reliable and speaks more quickly, gut has a more vivid tone colour.[23] A return to unwound gut strings in the upper reaches of the violin and cello has produced for at least one modern performer, 'more articulate attacks because of the almost inaudible chiff as the bow begins its motion ... The tone of the gut strings is richer in strong upper overtones, more complex and full than that of steel strings.'[24]

Vibrato

Until around 1900 vibrato in string playing was regarded as ornamental, and in the following decades its continuous employment gradually became a controversial issue. As late as 1921 Joachim's pupil Leopold Auer recommended sparing use of vibrato, which he said was 'an effect, an embellishment; it can lend a touch of divine pathos to the climax of a phrase or the course of a passage, but only if the player has cultivated a delicate sense of proportion in the use of it ... The excessive *vibrato* is a habit for which I have no tolerance, and I always fight against it when I observe it in my pupils – though often, I must admit, without success.'[25] This follows the advice in Joachim's *Violinschule*, which in turn cited Spohr's restraint and remarked: 'the pupil cannot be sufficiently warned against its habitual use, especially in the wrong place. A violinist whose taste is refined and healthy will always recognise the steady tone as the ruling one, and will use vibrato only where the expression seems to demand it.'[26] Joachim's five recordings of 1903 incorporate some long notes with no vibrato and others where it varies in intensity. Amongst other relevant evidence, the recording by the Flonzaley Quartet of the Brahms Piano Quintet reveals the use of vibrato on heavily accentuated notes and on pitches held for longer durations.

> Vibrato was also used continuously in cantabile passages. For example in a recording of Smetana's First Quartet by the Bohemian Quartet founded around 1892, the cantabile slow movement features vibrato on almost every pitch, though the normal mode of playing is non-vibrato in other movements. Similarly, recordings of players trained during the nineteenth century often feature continual vibrato for the 'singing' theme (often the second theme) in a sonata-allegro movement.[27]

Vibrato acquired its modern status at the hands of players trained in France and Belgium rather than in Germany. Wieniawski (1835–80),

Vieuxtemps (1820–81), Ysaÿe (1853–1931) and Kreisler (1875–1963) were an important influence here; the last two made recordings which prove the point. It seems certain that once the Brahms Clarinet Quintet was performed regularly outside the Joachim circle, the style of violin playing applied to it must have changed radically from what Brahms originally heard, reflecting the wide variety of approaches to the instrument in the years following his death. Various editions of *Grove's Dictionary* bear witness to such a change, *Grove 2* (1904–10) reprinting an article from *Grove 1* (1879–89): 'When the vibrato is really an emotional thrill it can be highly effective ... but when, as is too often the case, it degenerates into a mannerism, its effect is either painful, ridiculous, or nauseous, entirely opposed to good taste and common sense'. By the time of *Grove 3* (1927–8) the earlier attack on vibrato is characteristically replaced with: 'As an emotional effect produced by physical means it has obvious dangers, but no string-player's technique is complete without its acquirement'. At the same time, Flesch could write, 'If we consider the celebrated violinists of our day, it must be admitted that in every case they employ an uninterrupted (though technically unobjectionable) vibrato'.[28]

Portamento

Another important area of performance practice in string playing is the use of portamento, a conspicuous slide between positions as an expressive device. Portamenti served to shape the melody by calling attention to certain structurally important pitches. This was already a prominent feature of the technique of some violinists well before 1800 and subsequently found its way into orchestral playing, early recordings reflecting a well-established approach. Its vocal nature was emphasised by Joachim: 'As a means borrowed from the human voice ... the use and manner of executing the portamento must come naturally under the same rules which hold good in vocal art'.[29] Flesch recalled the poetic quality which could be achieved in Joachim's portamenti, while regretting their accompanying crescendi and diminuendi.[30] Portamento plays a significant part in Joachim's two 1903 recordings of his arrangements of Brahms's Hungarian Dances and this is typical of its period;[31] Marie Hall's 1916 recording of an abridged Elgar Violin

Concerto under the composer's direction has more portamenti in both solo and orchestral parts than was ever the case subsequently.[32] The dangers of over-indulgence were consistently emphasised (e.g. by Leopold Auer), though the effect was clearly meant to be audible; undoubtedly, musical taste in Brahms's day set quite different norms from our own.

Finson analysed the use of portamento in ensemble from a recording of Beethoven's Op. 18 no. 4 by the Rosé Quartet, who played with Mühlfeld and gave some early performances of the Clarinet Quintet:

> In a sense, the performer provides the listener with an analysis of the melody by using the ornament to accentuate high notes and herald suspensions and cadences. Far from being an example of slovenliness in execution, the portamento shows the care and thoughtfulness applied to the musical text by nineteenth-century string players. The recording by the Rosé Quartet also reminds us that the portamento was used very seldom by good musicians. If the ornament was to be effective in articulating melodic shape to the listener, it could not be employed often.[33]

Identification of contexts appropriate to the portamento in unrecorded works poses difficulties; for all the detail given by Carl Flesch in *The Art of Violin Playing*, recordings 'reveal no regular practice in this regard'.[34]

Tempo flexibility, articulation and nuance

Aside from tonal elements, the principal stylistic areas for a study of Brahms's performance practice are tempo flexibility, articulation and nuance. All these must have been important interpretative features when the Quintet was first performed; after all, it was principally as an artist that Mühlfeld was admired by Brahms and his circle. As we have already implied, his performances were given at a time when musical tempo was considerably more flexible than it is today, and fluctuations in the surface rhythm of individual passages as well as in basic pulse for longer passages were common.

It is in this context that evidence of the playing of both Brahms and Joachim must be considered. In relation to tempo modification Brahms made the oft-quoted remark that it should be applied 'con discrezione', a comment which nowadays certainly needs to be read in terms of the prevailing aesthetic. On the metronome, Brahms made it clear that tempo in his music could not be constant: 'I have never believed that my blood and a mechanical instrument go very well together'.[35] Recorded evidence from the early twentieth century suggests that individual subjects in sonata form were assigned their own tempi, connected by transitional passages; unstable areas in the development and coda often featured accelerating tempi to heighten tension and drama when appropriate. Brahms's more general advice to at least one player is revealing; 'Machen Sie es wie Sie wollen, machen Sie es nur schön' ('Do it how you like, but make it beautiful'). This is a telling remark in the context of a tradition dating back at least as far as Maczewski's article in *Grove 1* (1879), which emphasised the intellectual (rather than technical) qualities of Brahms's piano playing. Broadening the overall picture, Clara Schumann's pupil Fanny Davies (1861–1934), who premièred the piano parts of Brahms's clarinet works in England (the composer being unwilling to travel), left the following reminiscence of Brahms's own playing. It comes at the end of Tovey's article on Brahms in *Cobbett*, many of whose contributors were personally acquainted with Brahms and his circle:

Brahms's manner of interpretation was free, very elastic and expansive; but the balance was always there – one felt the fundamental rhythms underlying the surface rhythms. His phrasing was notable in lyric passages. In these a strictly metronomic Brahms is as unthinkable as a fussy or hurried Brahms in passages which must be presented with adamantine rhythm. Behind his often rugged, and almost sketchy playing, there never failed to appear that routined and definite school of technique without which he might sometimes have become almost a caricature of himself. When Brahms played, one knew exactly what he intended to convey to his listeners: aspiration, wild fantastic flights, majestic calm, deep tenderness without sentimentality, delicate, wayward humour, sincerity, noble passion. In his playing, as in his music and in his character, there was never a trace of sensuality.

His touch could be warm, deep, full, and broad in the *fortes*, and not hard even in the *fortissimos*; and his *pianos*, always of carrying power, could be as round and transparent as a dewdrop. He had a wonderful legato. He belonged to that racial school of playing which begins its phrases well, ends them well, leaves plenty of space between the end of one and the beginning of another, and yet joins them without any hiatus. One could hear that he listened very intently to the inner harmonies, and of course he laid great stress on good basses.

Like Beethoven, he was most particular that his marks of expression (always as few as possible) should be the means of conveying the inner musical meaning. The sign < >, as used by Brahms, often occurs when he wishes to express great sincerity and warmth, applied not only to tone but to rhythm also. He would linger not on one note alone, but on a whole idea, as if unable to tear himself away from its beauty. He would prefer to lengthen a bar or phrase rather than spoil it by making up the time into a metronomic bar.

Thus it appears that Brahms's tempo modification was related to context as much as to degree. A knowledge of harmony was important to interpreting his music, as was controlled flexibility. Brahms was perhaps more welcoming of sensuousness from the clarinet than he might have been from his own piano playing. Schauffler noted that Brahms attended a rehearsal by the Soldat-Röger Quartet, at which he was so touched by the Clarinet Quintet that tears came to his eyes.[36] To cover his emotion he marched across the room, closed the first-violin part and growled, 'Stop the terrible music!'

According to a member of his quartet, Joachim also had a spontaneous and unpredictable approach to tempo: 'to play with him is damned difficult. Always different tempi, different accents'.[37] Cobbett described him as 'warm and temperamental, with spontaneous impulses, trusting always to the inspiration of the moment, but controlled always by a wonderful sense of style, and an almost uneasy mastery of the art of rubato playing'.[38] In terms of accentuation Joachim won high praise from his biographer, J. A. Fuller Maitland, who observed that his regulated or logical freedom was based on the principle of the agogic accent, i.e.,

The kind of accent that consists, not of an actual stress or intensification of tone on the note, but of a kind of lengthening out of its time value, at the beginning of the bar, and at points where a secondary accent may be required. All the greatest interpreters of the best music have been accustomed to play this kind of accent on the first note of the bar, or of a phrase, as taste may suggest, but none have ever carried out the principle so far or with such fine results as Joachim has done.[39]

Articulation is discussed at length in Joachim's *Violinschule*. His colleague Andreas Moser drew the traditional analogy with rhetoric, but for cantabile passages implied a seamless legato; naturally, this would not have been expected in more vigorous music.[40] It is clear from a correspondence between Brahms and Joachim in 1879 that Brahms followed Classical composers in regarding the shortening of the second of a pair of notes as obligatory (though during his lifetime this was no longer universally taken for granted), whereas in longer phrases it was optional. A famous occurrence of paired quavers of this type occurs during the approach to the middle section of the Adagio of the Clarinet Quintet (bar 47).

Like many of his contemporaries, Brahms notated legato by means of a series of smaller-scale slurs which correspond to string bowings, but whose intent and meaning in various contexts remained ambiguous throughout the nineteenth century. There was no longer the eighteenth-century expectation that the slur indicated an expressive accent followed by diminuendo; such characteristics might well be directly contradicted by the musical sense. Brymer draws an analogy between Brahms's phrasing of his clarinet parts and string bowing, proposing between slurs 'just a gentle brush of the tongue ... or no sort of tongue-action at all, if it is felt that this is more natural'.[41] But even within legato passages it seems probable that today's clarinettists employ a smaller range of articulations than Mühlfeld, with nuance determined less evidently by the harmony. However, perhaps Brahms's slurs (and their implied rhetorical connotations) should not be quite so readily dismissed. Having analysed the use of rubato by the Flonzaley Quartet in the scherzo of Brahms's Piano Quintet, Finson concludes:

> [it] is not only an expressive device meant to intensify the drive of this pressing scherzo but also an articulatory strategy which highlights the repetition of motivic ideas. The modern performer's stereotype of Brahms's music, that it consists of long uninterrupted phrases, runs totally contrary to the practice of performers trained during his lifetime. In the surviving recordings these contemporary musicians use every expressive means at their command to separate melodic and motivic units from one another in Brahms's music, revealing his penchant for composing continually developing variations.[42]

In describing his own project to perform Brahms's sonatas for violin and for cello and one of the piano trios, Finson firstly mentions his use of historical instruments, removal of continuous vibrato and reinstatement of portamento. 'Moreover, use of short phrasing units, rubato, and tempo modification lent rhetorical variety to individual themes and heightened dramatic contrasts to whole movements which realized the expressive potential in Brahms's music and revealed the presence of emotional qualities seldom heard in the rather mechanical performances we normally hear.'[43] In Brahms's day the most intense appeal to the sentiments and emotions was made through the intellect. As Finson observes, 'The practice consists not so much of rigid requirements as of flexible strategies manipulated to express the view of a particular artist. In a music such as Brahms's, intended for multiple performances over an extended period of time, this performing practice could only be a virtue.'

Later interpretations

Interpretations of the Brahms Clarinet Quintet on record during the twentieth century have displayed various degrees of elegance and passion.[44] The two abridged movements recorded in 1917 by Charles Draper remained in the catalogue until 1925; the tempo is rather slow and there is considerable indulgence in rubato and vibrato by the string players.[45] The clarinet tone is firm and direct. In 1926 appeared Frederick Thurston's recording for the National Gramophone Society, with the Spencer-Dyke Quartet. Although praised (especially for its clarinet tone), Thurston's acoustic recording was remaindered by 1928 and a new electric recording by Charles Draper and the Léner Quartet appeared the following year. One reviewer wrote, 'Brilliant though the present performance is, there can be no doubt that the NGS (i.e. Thurston) is in closer contact with the Brahms.'[46] The sheer flexibility of Draper's performance certainly offers food for thought; furthermore, it seems that Mühlfeld heard Draper play the work during the early years of the century and told the British clarinettist that his interpretation had revealed subtleties in the work which Mühlfeld himself had not observed.[47]

In 1932 the Italian Luigi Amodio recorded the Quintet with the

Poltronieri Quartet.[48] 1937 witnessed one of the most celebrated interpretations of all: that by Reginald Kell and the Busch Quartet (HMV
DB 3383–6). Kell was the foremost pupil of Charles Draper's nephew,
Haydn Draper. *The Gramophone* reported that the Busch Quartet's
playing was 'of superlatively high quality and here reaches an even
higher standard, which goes to make up a well-nigh perfect interpretation. With all these virtues the clarinettist, Reginald Kell, must
unreservedly be associated. His instrument has never sounded more
beautiful than in this recording ... Perhaps some people may consider
Mr Kell's restraint excessive, but I shall not agree with them'. Kell's
individuality, freedom and use of vibrato invites comparison with
Mühlfeld, though not his restraint. Robert Philip has noted that in the
1930s Kell's vibrato was unique and that his style contrasted vividly
with that of the traditional clarinet school. 'His phrasing is extremely
flexible, with detailed dynamic nuances, a wide dynamic range, and a
vibrato which varies in prominence from one note to another.'[49] The
playing of Adolf Busch and his colleagues presents an even more
complete link with the past. Busch was born in the year of composition
of the Quintet and his teachers at the Cologne Conservatory – Willy
Hess and Bram Eldering – were both pupils of Joseph Joachim, whose
death in 1907 deprived Busch of the opportunity to study with him.[50]
Busch's mastery of rubato and portamento, together with his glorious
phrasing, surely offer a glimpse of Brahms's intentions, at least in
relation to the string quartet.

From the early post-war era came LPs from Alfred Gallodoro
(transferred from 78s), Kell (with the Fine Arts Quartet), Leopold
Wlach and Alfred Boskovsky. Reviewers began to argue in favour of
one recording or another; Kell's second disc was described as 'by no
means the ideal performance', whilst Wlach 'does not show quite as
much imagination as we hoped'. Boskovsky won special praise from
the critics, who also liked his second version from 1962, despite a
suggested lack of intensity of feeling. In this year there were also
recordings from Kell (with a reconstituted Fine Arts Quartet), David
Oppenheimer and Jost Michaels. In 1963 a new version from Heinrich
Geuser and the Drolc Quartet won many friends, even in the face of
later competition from Gervase de Peyer (1965) and Vladimír Říha
(1966). *The Monthly Letter* reported that 'here at last is a really satisfy-

ing performance of the Brahms. The clarinettist not only makes a beautiful sound but is obviously inspired by the string quartet to play with the utmost sensitivity.' During the next decade a fascinating variety of stylistic approaches were displayed by Jack Brymer (1968), Karl Leister (1969), Yona Ettlinger, Robert Gugolz and Oskar Mich-allik (1972) and Herbert Stähr (1973). British players were prominent in the avalanche of interpretations which followed, but this is a corner of the repertory where national styles have always been readily compared and contrasted. But experience with boxwood clarinets designed well before Mühlfeld's time prompts one to question whether the Boehm- (or even the modern German-) system clarinet can successfully match his original range of colours, despite their increased dynamic capacity.

7

The legacy of Brahms's clarinet music

Introduction: clarinet music after Brahms

After the brilliant creations of Brahms and Reger, public interest in the clarinet as a chamber music instrument seemed to become strangely paralysed. But today, thanks to the efforts of outstanding players and chamber music circles, the clarinet has regained its rightful place in the concert hall, especially as the radio has for many years made wide use of the solo player. Numerous works with solo clarinet have been written in recent decades, and most of them far exceed the level of the average work composed at the turn of the century...

So wrote the German clarinettist Oscar Kroll in a book which was in preparation during the 1930s.[1] At the beginning of the twentieth century the most enduring composers for the clarinet seem to have been those with their own individual mode of expression rather than subscribers to the Brahms tradition. In radically expanding the clarinet's expressive range, Berg caused surprise and astonishment with his *Vier Stücke* Op. 5 (1913), damned with faint praise in Tuthill's article in *Cobbett* as 'Very *outré*; interesting as studies in effects'. Meanwhile, the French school continued to flourish in its own distinctive vein, Debussy contributing a masterly and taxing example of the *solo de concours* with his *Première rapsodie* of 1910. The solo clarinet repertory was also soon to be imbued with jazz influence (Stravinsky) and neo-classical traits (Krenek and others).

The influence of Brahms

More variable in musical quality were the various excursions into the genres of the clarinet sonata, trio and quintet cultivated by German and Austrian composers in the years immediately following Brahms's death. His intoxicating cocktail of lyrical and dramatic elements within a closely argued structure eluded most entrants in the arena. The Sonata Op. 5 in G by Brahms's pupil Gustav Jenner was dedicated to Mühlfeld and is closely modelled on his teacher's F minor Sonata and Clarinet Trio. By comparison with many of his contemporaries Jenner produced thematic material which is both idiomatic and suitable for development, notwithstanding a somewhat feeble finale. The clarinet trio as a genre also maintained some momentum; Alexander Zemlinsky's Op. 3 was published in the year of Brahms's death, whilst Wilhelm Berger's Op. 94 (1905), written for the trio in which he played with Mühlfeld, has already been noted in Chapter 4.[2] Mühlfeld's repertory also included trios by Rudolf Braun and by Leo Schrattenholz.[3]

Examination of the many clarinet quintets composed after Brahms serves to enhance rather than diminish appreciation of his achievement, successful excursions into the territory remaining rare. A well-integrated texture remained a fearsome challenge, while truly idiomatic clarinet writing also eluded many. In his advice to composition students in 1913 Thomas Dunhill observed that there had been great mechanical improvements to wind instruments facilitating chromatic scales, but that problems in relation to tone-colour and balance remained as they were in Mozart's time. The increased executive possibilities exposed the composer to new dangers, all too easily inducing idioms that were certainly possible but nevertheless unsuitable.[4] Representative of the very dry quintets written by certain German composers is the Clarinet Quintet Op. 19 by Stephan Krehl, dedicated to Mühlfeld and published by Simrock in 1902.[5] Here the superficial similarities with Brahms are overwhelming: scored for A clarinet, the work follows its predecessor's formal outlines, with a first movement in compound time, followed by a 3/4 Lento with 2/4 middle section, an Allegretto grazioso leading to a Vivace, and a theme and variations as finale. But the melodic and dramatic inspiration underlying the Brahms is sadly lacking.

Max Reger

Virtually all the chamber music written in Germany, Austria and England at this period failed to achieve Brahms's international recognition and did not travel within Europe in subsequent years. This is even true of a composer of the stature of Max Reger, who extended the possibilities of tonality without discarding its framework and whose individual idiom brought him much hostility as well as widespread recognition and imitation. Reger wrote his two Clarinet Sonatas Op. 49 (1900) after hearing a performance of Brahms's F minor Sonata by the local clarinettist Johann Kürmeyer and his own teacher in Weiden, Adalbert Lindner.[6] Reger premièred his later large-scale Sonata Op. 107 with Julius Winkler of Darmstadt in 1909. A few days after starting work on it, he wrote: 'it will be an uncommonly clear work; you can't allot overmuch "technique" to a wind player because there is always a danger of the chamber music style going by the board and the whole thing becoming a concertino, which would be too bad. Brahms has set a pattern for what the style should be'.[7]

Reger's Clarinet Quintet Op. 146 is dedicated to Karl Wendling, whose quartet had often played with Mühlfeld; after his death they collaborated with Philipp Dreisbach (1891–1980) of Stuttgart, premièring the work together in 1916. Many critics would agree with Kroll that the Quintet is Reger's crowning achievement: 'the whole work flows serenely and lovably in harmonious contentment and ends with variations bubbling over with ideas'.[8] Restrained in character, Reger's Quintet treats the clarinet less idiomatically than Brahms, but in a way which integrates with the strings to an even greater extent. His melancholy colour and assured handling of the instruments are counterbalanced by a dense, chromatic texture, even in the final variations. Melodic ideas are often motivic, forming part of a texture and without Brahms's overt lyricism, except in contexts such as the work's very opening – which promises much – and in the trio of the Vivace. In the concert hall performances have taken place mainly in Germany; recently, British interest had ebbed to such an extent that a performance as late as 1984 could be claimed as the UK première, admittedly without any justification.[9]

Robert Fuchs and his contemporaries

Another outstanding and original clarinet quintet is the Op. 102 (1914, published 1919) of Robert Fuchs, teacher at the Vienna Conservatory from 1875 until 1911 and a friend of Brahms, from whom he received much encouragement as a composer. The Quintet met with an enthusiastic reception when it formed the centrepiece of one of his seventieth birthday concerts, but in common with his other works has never been widely known outside Austria.[10] Brahms was seldom enthusiastic about other composers, but in 1891 remarked that Fuchs was a splendid musician: 'everything is so fine, so skilful, so charmingly invented, that one always has pleasure in it'.[11] Fuchs counted among his pupils Mahler, Schreker, Schmidt, Sibelius and Zemlinsky. He was strongly influenced by the music of Schubert, whose facility in modulation he inherited. The Clarinet Quintet inhabits a sound-world related to Brahms and Reger, but distinguished noticeably by his use of Bb rather than A clarinet. The work nicely illustrates his lyrical gifts allied to a strong grasp of harmonic and contrapuntal technique, enabling him to continue the tradition of Brahms (though not at the same inspired level), without the stylistic innovations wrought by many of his contemporaries.

Other Austro-German clarinet quintets composed before the end of World War II included those by Hans Stieber (1920), Ewald Straesser (1920), Paul Hindemith (1923), Franz von Hoesslin, Gunther Raphael (1924), Kurt Schubert (1925), Siegfried Müller (1927), Egon Kornauth (1931), Frida Kern (1933), Joseph Lederer (1941), Ilse Fromm-Michaels (1944) and Karl Höller (c. 1944–6). The influence of Brahms continued into the 1950s in the quintet by the Viennese émigré Egon Wellesz. Brahms's biographer Hans Gál contributed an even later example, his Op. 107 (1978); he had studied with Mandyczewski at Vienna University during the period 1908–13. But of all these quintets after Reger and Fuchs, only the Hindemith (requiring both Eb and Bb clarinets) has retained a foothold in the repertory and even this work had to wait thirty years before it was published. From elsewhere in Europe came quintets by Charles de Balorre (1906), Henri Marteau (1909), Jaroslav Rídky (1926) and Albert Moeschinger (1943). Mátyás Seiber's *Concertino* (1926–8) was originally a divertimento for clarinet quintet. The Russian Alexander Krein published two *Esquisses hébraïques* for the medium (c. 1910–1914). Scandinavian quintets were written by Edvin Kallstenius (1930) and J. L. Emborg (1931). The Israeli Paul Ben Haim wrote a quintet in 1941, whilst American quintets included those by Otto Luening (1921), Quincy Porter (1929), Burnet Tuthill (1936), Edward Burlinghame Hill (1940) and Sam Gardner (*Hebrew Rapsodie*), all of which remained in manuscript; the *Prefatio brevis* for quintet by Robert Mills Delaney was published in 1940.

The clarinet quintet in England

Brahms's influence upon English composers was of special significance. After a performance of Brahms's Quintet in 1895 at the Royal College of Music in London, Stanford challenged his composition class to write a similar work. The twenty-year-old Samuel Coleridge-Taylor rose to the occasion with his highly individual and rhythmically complex Quintet Op. 10 in F sharp minor, which was later played by none other than Mühlfeld, was published by Breitkopf and Härtel in 1906 and won for him wide recognition as a composer. Oscar Street noted ten years later that Coleridge-Taylor had falsified the prophecy of an 'eminent musician' at the College, who had declared that no composer could write for this combination without showing Brahms's influence:

> The quintet is a work of absolute originality, and bears no resemblance to Brahms from beginning to end, unless it be in the masterly way in which both composers, each in his different style, have blended the clarinet-tone with the strings. Coleridge-Taylor's quintet deserves to be far better known than it is; it is the only one (and a good many others have been written) that in my opinion deserves a place alongside those of Mozart and Brahms.[12]

A hundred years later, this quintet may be seen to owe something to Brahms, if only through the tutelage of Stanford, who was himself a devotee. For all its individuality (not least the chalumeau coloration of the main theme of the Adagio), its use of the A clarinet and the presence of certain cyclical elements invite some comparison with Brahms's Quintet.[13]

The revival of the Elizabethan 'fancy' – a one-movement form in several sections – had been the subject of considerable discussion in Stanford's book *Musical Composition: a Short Treatise for Students*

(London, 1911), and his interest in this rhapsodic form bore fruit in the work of many of his pupils. His favourite student was Herbert Howells, whose *Rhapsodic Quintet* (Stainer & Bell, 1921) is one of his very finest pieces, albeit a mere eleven minutes in length. The title belies a tightly knit structure and the work has a characterful individuality which few composers after Brahms were able to match. Marion Scott noted in *Cobbett* that the Quintet was written with sensitive appreciation of instrumental needs, but that it was difficult to interpret because the characteristic traits of several styles of writing were closely combined. She made the perceptive observation that it was beautiful in an unusual and unworldly way.

The lyrical yet dramatic potential of the clarinet quintet medium manifestly suited the style of English music, and late in his life Stanford himself was finally tempted to the genre by the example of Howells, writing his two Fantasies in 1921 and 1922; they remained unpublished and were actually lost sight of until relatively recently. Stanford had already shown the influence of the Adagio of Brahms's Quintet in the *Caoine* of his Clarinet Sonata; in the Fantasies he produced another specialised reconciliation of Irish character with the Austro-German tradition of craftsmanship, without emulating the formal discipline or inspiration of Brahms.

Other British composers for clarinet quintet included Arthur Somervell (*c.* 1913), Joseph Holbrooke (two quintets, 1914), Cyril Scott (1925), York Bowen (1932),[14] Ralph Walter Wood (1937) the émigré Franz Reizenstein (1937) and Ruth Gipps (1942).

Somervell provides an interesting link between the English and German schools, His studies with Stanford at Cambridge and with Parry at the Royal College of Music were interspersed with two years (1883–5) at the Berlin Hochschule, where his teachers were Friedrich Kiel and Woldemar Bargiel. Kiel had been Stanford's mentor and Bargiel was a disciple of Schumann and step-brother to Clara. Somervell's conservative style won him success for his vocal and choral music, but led to instant oblivion in the case of his instrumental music. His Quintet was premièred in London by Haydn Draper on 19 May 1919 and was then remembered as remaining in manuscript only via Rendall.[15] As in Stanford's Concerto, Somervell demands the use of both B♭ and A clarinets during the course of the piece, a feature which inevitably increases its practical difficulty.[16] Of later works the Quintet by Arthur Bliss (for A clarinet) is a work of striking personality, written for Frederick Thurston at a time when Bliss was rediscovering the forms and idioms of established tradition. He contrives a conversational lyricism, but with a wealth of thematic dovetailing and interrelationship. The heart of the work is its third movement, Adagietto espressivo, in which at least one writer has detected an eloquence comparable with Brahms in the manner in which the expressive and tonal range of the clarinet is explored.[17] The central section has an intensity and clarinet figuration which also readily calls Brahms to mind, though the tonal language and imitative writing remain characteristic of Bliss. Of well-integrated works for clarinet quintet, this would be the preference (besides Mozart and Brahms) of most British players. Later composers have continued to be inspired by the medium, including Gordon Jacob (1946), William Wordsworth (1952), Geoffrey Bush (1953), Benjamin Frankel (1956), Arnold Cooke (1962), Elisabeth Maconchy (1963), Robert Simpson (1968) and Iain Hamilton (1976), as well as a large number of writers of a younger generation.

During the twentieth century the clarinet has enjoyed an enhanced status in many different types of music, its expressive qualities and agility utilised by a wide range of composers.[18] It could be argued that this variety of styles and idioms might well have rediscovered the clarinet as a recital and chamber instrument without the partnership of Brahms and Mühlfeld, but there can be no doubt that Brahms's encounter with the clarinet acted as an immense influence and stimulus to later composers of different nationalities and styles.

A list of Brahms's chamber music

Opus no.	Title	Date of composition
	Scherzo, c, vn, pf	1853
8	Pf trio, B	1853–4, R/1889
18	Sextet (str), B♭	1858–60
25	Pf quartet, g	1861
26	Pf quartet, A	1861–2
34	Pf quintet, f	1861–4
36	Sextet (str), G	1864–5
38	Vc sonata, e	1862–5
40	Hn trio, E♭	1865
51	Str quartets, c, a	c. 1865–73
60	Pf quartet, c	1855–75
67	Str quartet, B♭	1876
78	Vn sonata, G	1878–9
87	Pf trio, C	1880–2
88	Str quintet, F	1882
99	Vc sonata, F	1886
100	Vn sonata, A	1886
101	Pf trio, c	1886
108	Vn sonata, d	1886–8
111	Str quintet, G	1890
114	Clt trio, a	1891
115	Clt quintet, b	1891
120	Clt sonatas, f, E♭	1894

Appendix 2

A review of the first London performance, The Times, *29 March 1892*

On 28 March 1892 at one of the 'Popular Concerts' at St James's Hall, Richard Mühlfeld introduced Brahms's Clarinet Quintet to London, with Joseph Joachim, Louis Ries, Ludwig Straus and Alfredo Piatti. The audience included Grove, Parry and Stanford. On that occasion Joachim, 'apparently to counterbalance the extreme novelty of the opening piece', gave as his solos the Barcarolle and Scherzo by Spohr, with 'his own pretty Romance in B flat' as an encore. The final concerted number was Mozart's Trio in B flat, with pianist Miss Agnes Zimmermann, who also played Schumann's G minor Sonata. Mlle Gherlsen, a pupil of Georg Henschel, sang Mozart's 'Deh vieni non tardar' and Brahms's 'Feldeinsamkeit' and 'Vergebliches Ständchen' (the last in a French translation); the critic observed that 'her agreeable voice and good method have been more favourably exhibited on former occasions'.

The chief event of the present musical season took place last night in the production, in circumstances the most favourable that can be imagined, of the quintet for clarinet and strings lately written by Brahms. In the case of a work of such incontestable genius it is useless to withhold expressions of admiration until after a second hearing; the form in which it is written is, besides, so clear that its general scope and drift need hardly overtax the powers of the merest tyro to appreciate. The quality which first strikes the hearer is that of homogeneity. The key, B minor, is hardly departed from during the whole work, the thematic material is welded together by the use of a phrase which appears in various modifications, in nearly every section, and, finally, the disposition of the instruments is so skilful that the tone of the wind instruments [*sic*], instead of standing apart from that of the strings, seems merely to complete their volume and perfect their quality. The phrase referred to is prominent throughout the first movement, in the closing bars of which it is worked up to a most exciting climax; in the exquisitely melodious and original adagio, in which the strings are muted, it is evidently the formation of an extraordinary passage of what may be called declamation for the clarinet, a passage unmistakably Hungarian in colouring; and it makes a last appearance at the close of the finale, a theme with variations. Here, as the end approaches, the figure of six semiquavers of which the phrase consists is gradually more and more closely copied until it is introduced in its original form, yet with such art that it is hardly to be distinguished from a culminating variation. The third movement is a lovely andantino, on one of those deliciously winning melodies of which the Viennese master has a monopoly; this leads to the *presto non assai* which stands in the place of a scherzo, and which is decorated with quaint flourishes for all the instruments in turn, such as give character in some analogous movements in Brahms's later works, for example, the trio in C minor and the third violin sonata. The delay in publishing the work and its companion piece, a trio for pianoforte, clarinet and violoncello, to be played on Saturday next, has had very happy results in the engagement of the clarinet-player who had the honour of playing them under the composer's direction, and the adoption, for that player's convenience, of the Continental pitch. Herr Mühlfeld is a superlatively fine artist, and not only his tone, but the perfection of his phrasing, the depth of his musical expression and his absolute ease and finish, mark him as a player altogether without parallel in England at least. His broad delivery of the declamatory passage in the adagio won him special honour at the close of the movement, and it was not a mere act of courtesy on the part of Dr Joachim to suggest to the newcomer that he should acknowledge the reception. The famous quartet were at their best, which is equivalent to saying the work was given in perfection. In particular Signor Piatti's exquisite playing in the first variation of the finale deserves a word of remark.

The mechanism of Mühlfeld's Baermann-Ottensteiner clarinets

(L = left hand, R = right hand, th = thumb , finger 1 = index)

Some technical details

(A) Configuration of the late eighteenth-century five-keyed clarinet: *keys in order of development:*

{	(1) *a'*	L1
{	(2) speaker	Lth
	(3) *e/b'*	L4
	(4) *ab/eb"*	R4
	(5) *f#/c#"*	L4

(B) Iwan Müller's *Clarinette Omnitonique* (1812) added the following keys: *from top of the instrument:*

(6) *g#'*	L1
(7) *eb'/bb"*	L3
(8) *c#'/g#"*	L4
(9) *a'/b'* trill	R1
(10) *f'/c'''*	L1
(11) *bb/f"*	R3
(12) *b/f#"*	R4
(13) *f/c"*	R4

Müller also provided alternative right-hand thumb touchpieces to keys (4) and (5)

(C) The Baermann–Ottensteiner clarinets used by Mühlfeld made playing much easier because, by means of auxiliary levers, most keys could be controlled from different positions or were provided twice over. Thus a lever soldered to the $c\sharp'/g\sharp''$ key made it workable by R1; $e\flat'/b\flat''$ was available from R1 as well as from L3; and with a new lever L3 or L4 could play f'/c'''. New $b\flat/f''$ and $a\flat/e\flat''$ levers were provided for L4 (the latter replacing Rth), also a second trill key for R1. Ring-key mechanisms corrected $f\sharp'/c\sharp'''$ and $b/f\sharp''$.[1] A Rth key was retained for $f\sharp/c\sharp''$. With fewer tone-holes, the Baermann system had a greater potential for resonance than either the subsequent German Oehler system, or the Boehm system which became popular elsewhere.

For detailed illustrations of Mühlfeld's clarinets, see Weston, *Clarinet Virtuosi of the Past*, plates 24 and 25; also *Clarinet & Saxophone* 14/1 (1989), front cover and pp. 26-7.

Notes

Preface

1 Philip Radcliffe, 'Brahms', *Grove's Dictionary of Music and Musicians*, 5th edn (London, 1954), I, p. 879.
2 May, *The Life of Johannes Brahms*, II, pp. 250–1.
3 Frisch, *Brahms and the Principle of Developing Variation*, p. xiii.
4 See especially Weston, 'Players and composers', in Lawson, ed., *The Cambridge Companion to the Clarinet*, pp. 92–106.
5 Kell, 'The clarinet music of Johannes Brahms', p. 5.
6 Mason, *The Chamber Music of Brahms*, pp. 220–1. Mason was himself composer of an idiomatic clarinet sonata, dating from 1920.
7 These wonderfully responsive instruments are the work of Werner Schwenk (of Tübingen) and Jochen Seggelke (of Bamberg).

1 The nineteenth-century clarinet and its music

1 See Albert Rice, *The Baroque Clarinet* (Oxford, 1992), and Lawson, 'Single reeds before 1750', in *The Cambridge Companion to the Clarinet*, pp. 1–15.
2 Daniel Schubart, *Ideen zu einer Ästhetik der Tonkunst* (Vienna, 1806), written in 1784–5.
3 See Lawson, *Mozart: Clarinet Concerto*, pp. 29–31.
4 For example, Gottfried Weber, *Versuch einer geordneten Theorie der Ton-setzkunst* (Mainz, 1817–21), noted that wind instruments became more shrill as they became higher pitched, and that wind and stringed instruments might therefore impart different character to a particular key.
5 For example, Backofen (Concertante for two clarinets), Spohr (Octet, Concerto No. 4) and Schumann (*Phantasiestücke*).
6 *Cobbett's Cyclopaedic Survey of Chamber Music*, II, 98.
7 Weber's *Grand Duo Concertant* carries no dedication but may have been written for Spohr's clarinettist Simon Hermstedt or for Johann Kotte of the Dresden orchestra.

8 Michael Bryant, 'The clarinet on record', in *The Cambridge Companion to the Clarinet*, p. 205, even suggests that Weber would have approved of an orchestral transcription, since 'it sits uncomfortably among better integrated works for the medium'.

9 Cited in Pamela Weston, *Clarinet Virtuosi*, p. 149.

10 See Notley, 'Brahms as liberal', p. 118.

11 E. Hanslick, *Geschichte des Concertwesens in Wien: aus dem Concertsaal* (Vienna, 1870), II, p. 397. Hanslick had not heard Orsi play, but had merely heard him praised. See Jo Rees-Davies 'The development of the clarinet repertoire', in *The Cambridge Companion to the Clarinet*, p. 216.

12 Rendall, 'The clarinet in England', pp. 61–2.

13 In *Cobbett's Cyclopaedic Survey of Chamber Music*, I, p. 280, Tuthill assesses it as 'Good as Greek atmosphere, and musically effective if shortened by judicious cuts'.

14 The Heap and Prout sonatas appeared in a 'recommendation of good concerted music ... worthy of being listed with Weber's Grand Duo op. 48 and Schumann's Fantasiestücke op. 73' in *Musical Opinion & Music Trade Review* of March 1893.

15 Tuthill, in *Cobbett's Cyclopaedic Survey of Chamber Music*, describes the d'Indy as 'a long work of intellectual beauty. Splendid slow movement. A big work by a master.' The Hartmann is dismissed as 'effectively written but too saccharine'.

16 Significantly, the Täglichsbeck is described by Tuthill, *ibid.*, I, p. 282, as 'old-fashioned'.

17 In addition to clarinets made for Müller personally, Weston, *Clarinet Virtuosi*, p. 156, notes that his system was manufactured by the following: Bischoff of Darmstadt; Gentellet of Paris; Simiot of Lyons; Schott of Mainz; Charles Sax of Brussels; Mahillon & Bachmann of Brussels; Wünnenberg of Cologne; E. Albert of Brussels; Geisler of Amsterdam.

18 These instruments incorporate one particular important addition to Sax's design: the so-called 'patent c♯' key provides an easy *e–f♯* and *b'–c♯"* transition, revolutionising the clarinet's fluency in music with more than a single sharp in the key-signature.

19 Although no date for Mühlfeld's purchase of his Ottensteiner clarinets has been established, Nicholas Shackleton and Keith Puddy, 'Mühlfeld's clarinets', p. 26, postulate a date of 1875.

20 The Oehler system is so different from the Boehm used elsewhere that it continues to be specified in German orchestral vacancies. For other German designs after Baermann, see Kroll, *The Clarinet*, pp. 40–5.

21 Shackleton, 'The development of the clarinet', in *The Cambridge Companion to the Clarinet*, p. 27.

22 Weston, *Clarinet Virtuosi*, p. 151.

23 Baermann had worked on a type of 'clarinette omnitonique' with the Munich maker Benedikt Pentenrieder until the latter's death in 1849. Baermann reckoned him the outstanding maker in the field and that 'this tireless and mechanically inventive brain sacrificed to his invention his nights and later his very life'. Waterhouse, *The New Langwill Index*, p. 297, suggests that there is evidence that he was responsible for much of the mechanism adopted on the later Baermann-Ottensteiner clarinet.

24 Jochen Seggelke, 'Die Baermann-Ottensteiner Klarinette', p. 2.

25 Waterhouse, *The New Langwill Index*, p. 288.

26 Shackleton and Puddy, 'Mühlfeld's clarinets'. Rendall's comment (*The Clarinet*, p. 105) that the Baermann clarinet was 'a crude, rather unimaginitive model' has not found broad approbation.

2 Brahms and the orchestral clarinet

1 Daniel J. Koury, *Orchestral Performance Practices in the Nineteenth Century: Size, Proportion and Seating* (Ann Arbor, 1986), p. 149.

2 *Ibid.*, p. 141. Incidentally, the orchestra performed standing, a customary practice throughout much of Germany at that time; see p. 175.

3 Robert Vollstedt, *Clarinettenschule zum Selbstunterricht* (Hamburg, n.d.), quoted in Birsak, *Die Klarinette*, p. 9.

4 See Hector Berlioz, *Grand traité de l'instrumentation et d'orchestration modernes Op. 10* (Paris, 1843), trans. M. C. Clarke as *A Treatise on Modern Instrumentation* (London, 1858), pp. 107–8, 113. In fact, the overtly feminine characteristics Berlioz imputes to the clarinet may well have influenced Brahms in his nicknaming of Mühlfeld, 'Fräulein Klarinette'.

5 François-Auguste Gevært, *Nouveau traité d'instrumentation* (Paris, 1885), p. 92.

6 Carl Baermann, *Vollständige Clarinett-Schule* (Offenbach, 1864–75), quoted by Birsak, *Die Klarinette*, pp. 18–19.

7 See Adam Carse, *The History of Orchestration* (London,1925/R1964), p. 229.

8 Brian Newbould, *Schubert and the Symphony: a New Perspective* (London, 1992), p. 28.

9 See MacDonald, *Brahms*, p. 243.

10 Reported in May, *The Life of Johannes Brahms*, I, pp. 220–1.

11 See Litzmann, *Letters*, p. 56: 'to my great joy she [the singer Frau Guhrau]

was accompanied by basset horns which had been obtained with great difficulty. I do not think any instrument blends more perfectly with the human voice.' This probably refers to the aria for *Le nozze di Figaro*, 'Al desio di chi t'adora' K577.

12 Macdonald, *Brahms*, p.104, calls it a 'self education in the art of orchestral scoring'.

13 Macdonald, *ibid*., p. 302, calls this symphony 'the one in which instrumental colour is most often enjoyed for its own sake as well as for structural point'.

14 Where P. A. Browne, *Brahms: the Symphonies* (London, 1933), p. 11, accuses Brahms of 'more or less conscious archaism' in his use of C clarinet here, I have argued (*The Cambridge Companion to the Clarinet*, p. 41) that it came 'at a stage in his career when mere convention could not have had any further influence on its presence'. On the other hand, the presence of low *e♭*s in bars 295 and 297 (a semitone lower than the normal range) during a passage added to the clarinet part by Brahms after the publication of the first edition raises the awkward question of whether this movement was actually ever played on C clarinets.

15 In this fourth movement Brahms writes staccato for both clarinets at the extreme low end of the instrument in bars 149–52, a rich, warm timbre which blends ideally with pizzicato strings. In the fifth movement, the clarinet solo in bar 8 begins in the chalumeau register.

16 At bars 36ff and 50ff of the sixth movement of the *German Requiem* occurs the rare texture of unison oboe and clarinet, related to similar contexts in Schubert's last two symphonies.

3 Brahms's chamber music before 1891

1 May, *The Life of Johannes Brahms*, I, p. 59.

2 Musgrave and Pascall, 'The string quartets op. 51 no. 1 in C minor and no. 2 in A minor', pp. 138–9.

3 Pascall, 'Ruminations', p. 697.

4 Jenner, *Johannes Brahms*, p. 60, cited by Frisch, *Brahms and the Principle of Developing Variation*, p. 34.

5 Pascall, 'Ruminations', p. 699, citing as examples the first movement of the B flat Sextet and the second of the A major Piano Quartet and the F major String Quintet.

6 Mason, *The Chamber Music of Brahms*, pp. 82–3.

7 This slow movement has been widely associated with the death of

Brahms's mother in 1865. An important formal link with the clarinet music occurs in the central Molto meno allegro of the scherzo, which anticipates the equivalent context in the E flat Sonata Op. 120 no. 2 – and also looks back to the Piano Trio in B, Op. 8.

8 Mason, *The Chamber Music of Brahms*, p. 83.

9 Its première was given a year previously in Karlsruhe, with Brahms as pianist.

10 Mason, *The Chamber Music of Brahms*, pp. 88–9, where it is noted that Brahms composed over twenty string quartets before his first published example.

11 MacDonald, *Brahms*, p. 165.

12 Arnold Schoenberg, *Style and Idea*, ed. L. Stein (London, 1975), p. 401.

13 *Ibid.*, p. 290. Schoenberg claimed that a strict compositional style 'demands that nothing be repeated without promoting the development of the music, and that can only happen by way of far-reaching variations'. See Frisch, *Brahms and the Principle of Developing Variation*, p. 4.

14 See Frisch, *ibid.*, pp. 110–11, and Wilke, *Brahms, Reger, Schoenberg Streichquartette*, pp. 79–80, 82–4.

15 Ivor Keys, *Brahms Chamber Music*, pp. 30–1. In 1879 (well before the composition of the clarinet works) Maczewski had already written in *Grove 1* that there was a certain asceticism about Brahms's genius that was opposed to all that was merely pleasing to the ear. 'He does not court the understanding; he rather demands from it arduous and unwearied service.'

16 Musgrave, *The Music of Brahms*, p. 178.

17 *Brahms Briefwechsel* (Berlin, Deutsche Brahms-Gesellschaft), 1908–22, XII, p. 35.

18 Macdonald, *Brahms*, p. 342. The Double Concerto of 1887 had a lukewarm reception, even Brahms's friend Theodor Billroth confessing to Hanslick that he found the Concerto 'tedious and wearisome, a really senile production. If the *Zigeunerlieder* had not been composed later, one might almost believe it was all up with our Johannes! I do not know of a less important work of our good friend, and yet just this one is dear to his heart.'

19 The following commentary relating to Op. 111 is indebted to Musgrave, *The Music of Brahms*, pp. 206–8.

20 *Johannes Brahms: the Herzogenberg Correspondence*, ed. M. Kalbeck, trans. H. Bryant (London, 1909), pp. 386–96.

21 Cobbett, *Cobbett's Cyclopaedic Survey of Chamber Music*, I, p. 180.

22 Mason, *The Chamber Music of Brahms*, p. 202.

4 The genesis and reception of the Clarinet Quintet

1 Evans, *Handbook*, p. 264. Schauffler (*The Unknown Brahms*, p. 243) provides evidence that Brahms made the acquaintance of the Sinfonia Concertante K297b, at that time unequivocally ascribed to Mozart. In a letter from Meiningen to Clara Schumann (not included in Litzmann's selection) he wrote: 'My first morning in Meiningen I treated myself to a rehearsal and indeed I was the sole listener. When my noble hosts are here, the cry is Brahms and again Brahms. But I had the musicians play me a concerto for four winds by Mozart.'

2 See Litzmann, *Letters*, p. 196: 'You have never heard such a clarinet player as they have there in Mühlfeld. He is absolutely the best I know. At all events this art has, for various reasons, deteriorated very much. The clarinet players in Vienna and many other places are fairly good in orchestra, but solo they give one no real pleasure.'

3 Litzmann, *Letters*, pp. 146–7, where the translation of *grausamen* is perhaps a little harsh.

4 Margit L. McCorkle, *Werkverzeichnis*, p. 463.

5 Weston, *Clarinet Virtuosi*, pp. 209–35; see also 'Meine Primadonna – Brahms' Clarinettist', pp. 27–30. Much of the following biographical information on Mühlfeld derives from these sources. Mühlfeld's grandson Richard gave an address at the 1984 International Clarinet Congress in London.

6 Weston, *Clarinet Virtuosi*, p. 212, notes that Mühlfeld was given systematic violin teaching by the concert-master Friedhold Fleischauer and was taught music theory by the court conductor Emill Büchner.

7 Weston, *More Clarinet Virtuosi*, p. 204, notes that after the performance Richard Strauss (Meiningen's Kapellmeister for that winter) wrote to von Bülow that the work was 'very pretentiously scored, is a decoction of every conceivable coronation opera, in formal respect a hair-raising nonsense. For that reason, and played with great virtuosity by Mühlfeld, it will not fail to impress the public.' The concerto was never published.

8 Weston, *Clarinet Virtuosi*, p. 212.

9 Weston, 'Meine Primadonna', p. 27.

10 Geiringer, *Brahms*, p. 178.

11 Weston, *Clarinet Virtuosi*, p. 216, observes that 'Mühlfeld often spoke of this year, because the use of electric light in the theatre for the first time created a tremendous impression, and also because lines of light cavalry were drawn up in the forecourt to make a telling entrance for the audience'.

12 Rehearsals for the Trio began on the 21 November (with Joachim's cellist Robert Hausmann and Brahms), but rehearsals for the Quintet were delayed until the day of the concert itself, because of Joachim's commitments in Berlin. The Quintet was premièred with Joachim, Hausmann and two members of the Meiningen orchestra.

13 MacDonald, *Brahms*, p. 361.

14 Kross, 'The establishment of a Brahms repertoire', p. 34, has noted that in the case of the Clarinet Trio the usual priority given to performances of a new piece disappeared within two years, a process which may have been influenced by the grouping it requires: the violinist of a piano trio has to step back and make room for a clarinettist; the Quintet medium simply demands that an extra player be added to a pre-existing ensemble.

15 Musgrave, *The Music of Brahms*, p. 366.

16 *Grove 5*, 'Brahms', I, p. 879.

17 Geiringer, *Brahms*, p. 293.

18 May, *The Life of Johannes Brahms*, II, p. 250.

19 H. C. Colles, *Brahms* (London, 1908), p. 50.

20 Street, 'The clarinet and its music', p. 107.

21 Cobbett, *Cobbett's Cyclopaedic Survey of Chamber Music*, I, p. 180, where Tovey also states that he learned from Steinbach that the opening of the Trio had been intended for a fifth symphony.

22 Mason, *The Chamber Music of Brahms*, p. 222. Subsequent quotations here derive from his various comments on the Trio (pp. 219–30).

23 Musgrave, *The Music of Brahms*, p. 250.

24 Macdonald, *Brahms*, pp. 366–7. This is also the source for subsequent quotations in this paragraph.

25 Foster, *Brahms, Schenker and the Rules of Composition*, pp. 283–4.

26 See May, *The Life of Johannes Brahms*, II, pp. 249–50.

27 Weston, *Clarinet Virtuosi*, p. 218, notes that during the following days Mühlfeld became the centre of attraction and that a grand dinner was held in his honour, at which his place at table was decorated with the traditional laurels and also with two dolls for his children (Margarethe, *b.* 1883, and Hans, *b.* 1887).

28 In a programme note for his seventieth birthday concert in April 1996, Gervase de Peyer remembered performing the work in his youth to Georges Enesco, who had recalled the very first run-through of the work in a private house in the presence of Brahms. Enesco, who (as a little boy) had been concealed under the piano on this occasion, observed that the clarinettist had not been Mühlfeld.

29 Schauffler, Weston and others have noted that Brahms invited Steiner to

Mühlfeld's concert and paid him special attention at the gala dinner which followed.

30 Kross, 'The establishment of a Brahms repertoire', p. 34.
31 Letter of 30 December 1891 in Nora Bickley (trans.), *Letters from and to Joseph Joachim* (London, 1914), p. 445.
32 Cobbett, *Cobbett's Cyclopaedic Survey of Chamber Music*, I, p. 26.
33 Weston, *Clarinet Virtuosi*, p. 221.
34 Weston, *ibid.*, p. 261, and *More Clarinet Virtuosi*, pp. 94 and 338. She notes another verifiable performance by Egerton in 1898. Kross, 'The establishment of a Brahms repertoire', p. 34, notes three London performances in December 1892.
35 Bernard Shaw, *Music in London*, II, pp. 90–1; this review of 11 May 1892 proceeds to praise as charming and elegant the sextet for piano and wind by Ludwig Thuille, which was played in the same concert.
36 B. Litzmann, *Clara Schumann: an Artist's Life*, trans. Grace Hadow (London and Leipzig, 1913), II, p. 422.
37 Weston, *Clarinet Virtuosi*, p. 223, notes that on 7 May Dr Victor von Müller held a reception at his home, at which the guests included Brahms, Hausmann, Mühlfeld, Hanslick, Mandyczewski, the composer Ignaz Brüll, pianists Anton Door and Julius Epstein, and singers Joseph Gausbacher and Gustav Walter.
38 Weston, *ibid.*, p. 223. A photograph of Brahms and Mühlfeld at Berchtesgaden is reproduced in Weston, plate 23, and Lawson (ed.), *The Cambridge Companion to the Clarinet*, p. 98.
39 Litzmann, *Letters*, II, p. 266.
40 F. Schumann, 'Brahms and Clara Schumann', p. 508. Conversely, in 1933 Schauffler (*The Unknown Brahms*, p. 382) regarded the vehicle of Op. 120 as a distinct liability: 'When heard alone with a piano, the clarinet seldom sounds at its best. In the orchestra or in chamber music with strings it is far more magical.'
41 Musgrave, *The Music of Brahms*, pp. 251–2.
42 MacDonald, *Brahms*, p. 369.
43 Op. 120 was also arranged for violin, necessitating some alterations in the piano part. In the viola versions the piano part is unchanged.
44 Tovey, 'Brahms', in *Cobbett's Cyclopaedic Survey of Chamber Music*, I, p. 182.
45 Wife of Sir Charles Hallé from 1888: see Kross, 'The establishment of a Brahms repertoire', p. 34.
46 The prize-money was increased out of Brahms's own pocket and he arranged publication (by Simrock) of Rabl's piece.

47 Dates are of publication. Stanford's dedication to Mühlfeld of his Concerto Op. 80 was retracted because he never played it.

48 He performed in London, Bolton, Cambridge, Chislehurst, Helensburgh, Malvern, Manchester, Oxford and York. See Weston, *Clarinet Virtuosi*, p. 233. Mühlfeld's grandson reported that he gave a total of thirty-two concerts in London, more than in any other city outside Meiningen. An important source is his brother Christian's *Die herzogliche Hofkapelle in Meiningen* (Meiningen, 1910), which gives details of his concerts, repertory, reviews and colleagues.

49 The trio's concerts took place in Berlin, Jena, Kassel, Paris and Lyons. Weston, *Clarinet Virtuosi*, p. 233, notes that in 1905–6 Mühlfeld's own schedule included Marseilles, Lyons, Geneva and Paris.

50 The table in Kross, 'The establishment of a Brahms repertoire', p. 38, gives the following verifiable performances of the Quintet: 1891, 1; 1892, 22; 1893, 28; 1894, 7; 1895, 9; 1896, 5; 1897, 11; 1898, 4; 1899, 4; 1900, 6; 1901, 2; 1902, 3.

51 H. C. Colles, *Johannes Brahms* (London, 1908; 2nd edn, 1920).

52 Tovey, 'Brahms', in *Cobbett's Cyclopaedic Survey of Chamber Music*, I, p. 180.

53 Mason, *The Chamber Music of Brahms*, p. 231.

54 Bryant, 'The clarinet on record', pp. 206–7.

55 MacDonald, *Brahms*, p. 362.

5 Design and structure

1 Dyson, 'Brahms's Clarinet Quintet, Op. 115', p. 316, draws a parallel with the poignant falling thirds at the end of the last work Brahms wrote, the eleventh Chorale Prelude for organ.

2 Colles, *The Chamber Music of Brahms*, p. 59.

3 Homer Ulrich, *Chamber Music: the Growth and Practice of an Intimate Art* (New York, 1948), p. 332.

4 W. H. Hadow *Studies in Modern Music*, II (London, 1895), p. 283: Geiringer, *Brahms*, p. 337.

5 Cited by Evans, *Handbook*, p. 282.

6 For other major divergences between first edition and autograph, see the 1989 Breitkopf edition by Wolfgang Meyer.

7 Pascall, 'Formal principles', p. 99, where a parallel is drawn with the opening of Brahms's Cello Sonata, Op. 99.

8 Evans, *Handbook*, p. 284.

9 Graham, 'An analysis of Brahms' Quintet', p. 25, notes that this is not a

new device in his slow movements, citing the opening theme of the Third Symphony.

10 Dyson, 'Brahms's Clarinet Quintet, Op. 115', p. 317.

11 Evans, *Handbook*, p. 293. At the end of his commentary on p. 300 he contends that 'the last two movements of this quintet do not rise to the level of the others. It would be simple folly to attribute this to any falling off on the composer's part. It arises rather from his earnestness in writing suitably for his new protégé, and being thus led to the adoption of standards below his ideal.'

12 Amongst other movements of this type Pascall, 'Formal principles', p. 186, cites the finale of the C minor Symphony Op. 68, the Intermezzo in B flat Op. 76 no. 4 and *Geistliches Wiegenlied*, the second of the songs Op. 91 with viola.

13 Regarding the Presto non assai, the violinist Franz Kneisel remarked to a pupil, 'When I first played it for Brahms he said: "Would you please do me the favour of not taking that too fast?" He should have printed the *non assai* in capital letters.' See Schauffler, *The Unknown Brahms*, p. 411.

14 The last movement of the String Quartet Op. 67 has a total of eight variations plus coda following the theme. Schauffler, *The Unknown Brahms*, p. 411, remarks that although the themes are not at all alike, the Quintet's variations are an '*édition de luxe* of the youthful ones in the B flat sextet (Op. 18)'.

15 Graham, 'An analysis of Brahms' Quintet', p. 42.

16 Graham, *ibid.*, pp. 44–7, identifies this as a 'Brahms-motif', since it occurs so often in his work. He cites examples from the four symphonies, e.g. the opening of the second movement of No. 3.

17 Henry S. Drinker, *The Chamber Music of Johannes Brahms* (Philadelphia, 1932), p. 130.

18 For at least one writer, this variation has conjured up memories of the *Prometheus* theme in the finale of Beethoven's *Eroica* Symphony. See Schauffler, *The Unknown Brahms*, p. 411 fn.

6 Performance practice

1 Philip, *Early Recordings*, p. 229.

2 Philip, *ibid.*, p. 234.

3 Finson, 'Performing practice in the late nineteenth century', p. 457. He proceeds to argue that the performing practice of Brahms's time is neither arbitrary, slovenly, nor irrational, and that not surprisingly Brahms's music benefits when it is rendered in an authentic style.

4 As noted on page 46, the earliest recording comprises an abridged version of the Quintet's first two movements; it was made by Charles Draper and the London String Quartet during the summer of 1917.

5 As Robin Stowell observes in *The Cambridge Companion to the Violin*, p. 227, the three-volume *Violinschule* appears to have been written largely by Joachim's pupil, Andreas Moser.

6 Mühlfeld's grandson also noted that he was a monarchist rather than a democrat, recognising his professional debt to the Duke of Meiningen.

7 The earliest score to specify the use of clarinet vibrato is Glinka's *Trio Pathétique* (1832).

8 Brymer, *Clarinet*, p. 207.

9 In *Jahrbuch für musikalische Wissenschaft* 1 (1863), p. 22.

10 Arrey von Dommer, *H. C. Koch's Musikalisches Lexicon* (Heidelberg, 1865), p. 100.

11 In *Clarinet & Saxophone* 13/4 (1988), p. 10.

12 Donald Clark, 'Reflections on 14/1 (1989), Mühlfeld', p. 14. Bernard Shaw wrote in the early 1890s: 'In Germany clarionet-players use reeds which give a more strident, powerful, appealing tone than in England; and the result is that certain passages (in the Freischütz, for example) come out with a passion and urgency that surprises the tourist used to Egerton, Lazarus, or Clinton. But when it comes to the Parsifal Prelude or the second movement of Beethoven's Fourth Symphony, one misses the fine tone and dignified continence of the English fashion.' See *Music in London*, I, p. 96. Remarking upon German playing in general (III, p. 292) Shaw noted that 'except in the case of exceptionally fine players, who generally take the first chance of coming to England and settling here, the German woodwind player is content with a cheaper tone than the English one'.

13 Street, 'The clarinet and its music', p. 108.

14 Rendall, 'The clarinet in England', p. 78. Cf. his 1954 comment cited in Chapter 1, fn. 26.

15 Weston, *Clarinet Virtuosi*, p. 264. Clark, 'Reflections on Mühlfeld', cites the following colourful comment on Mühlfeld from one Johan Hock, cellist and conductor, who is listed in *Grove* and was resident in Birmingham for nearly fifty years until his death in 1946: 'He was not fit to lick Thurston's boots!'

16 Kenneth Hunt, 'Brahms and Mühlfeld: an anecdote', *Clarinet & Saxophone* 13/4 (1988), p. 13.

17 Baines, *Woodwind Instruments and their History* (London, 1957), p. 123.

18 Rendall, *The Clarinet*, p. 113.

19 In 1942 Rendall, 'The clarinet in England', p. 78, had noted that Mühlfeld's visits 'certainly gave a much needed fillip to clarinet players, to
composers too, even to musical journalists, who took the opportunity of
rediscovering the clarinet and writing some pretty nonsense about it. The
interest, however, was shortlived; by the end of the century the clarinettist was more or less where he was some ten years before.'

20 Weston, *Clarinet Virtuosi*, p. 210.

21 *Clarinet & Saxophone* 14/2 (1989), p. 7.

22 *Clarinet & Saxophone* 14/4 (1989), pp. 10–11. This ossia (bars 82–93 of
the movement) is retained in the Breikopf edition by Wolfgang Meyer.

23 Flesch, *The Art of Violin Playing*, I, pp. 10–11.

24 Finson, 'Performing practice', p. 463.

25 Leopold Auer, *Violin Playing as I Teach it* (London, 1921), pp. 22–4. The
term 'vibrato' incorporates a number of different techniques but is used
here in its now customary sense to indicate the more or less rapid oscilla-
tion of pitch.

26 Joachim and Moser, *Violinschule*, II, p. 96a.

27 Finson, 'Performing practice', p. 469.

28 Extracts from *Grove* editions and from Flesch are quoted from R. Philip,
'1900–1940', in *Performance Practice: Music after 1600* (London, 1989), p.
462.

29 *Violinschule*, II, p. 92.

30 *Violin Fingering*, p. 338. Flesch noted that this mannerism continued to
be taught at the Berlin Hochschule after 1907.

31 For an illustration of one such context, see Finson, 'Performing practice',
p. 466. For a detailed discussion of portamento see Flesch, *The Art of
Violin Playing*, I, pp. 28ff.

32 E.g. in Menuhin's 1932 recording with the composer, HMV DB1751–6.

33 Gramola, ES388–390 (matrix CK2822–2826). Arnold Rosé was described
by Flesch as playing in the style of the 1870s, 'with no concession to
modern tendencies in our art'. See Philip, *Early Recordings*, p. 236.

34 Finson, 'Performing practice', p. 465.

35 Letter to Georg Henschel quoted by Philip, *Early Recordings*, p. 218.

36 *The Unknown Brahms*, p. 180.

37 J. Levin in *Die Musik* (1926) quoted by Szigeti (1969) and cited by Philip,
Early Recordings, p. 218.

38 *Cobbett's Cyclopaedic Survey of Chamber Music*, II, pp. 38–9.

39 J. A. Fuller Maitland, *Joseph Joachim* (London and New York, 1905), pp.
29–30.

40 This distinction may be observed in Joachim's recordings of his *Romance in C* and in his arrangements of the Brahms Hungarian Dances.

41 Brymer, *Clarinet*, pp. 162–3.

42 Finson, 'Performing practice', p. 473. Joseph Bloch of the Budapest Conservatory, in *Methodik des Violinspiels und Violinunterrichts* (Strasburg, [1903]), p. 347, notes: 'The main point of phrasing is to make the work more understandable to the listeners. Phrasing results in the separation of individual parts, from which one can clearly recognize and distinguish the melodic members which have developed out of a pre-existent motive from those which are totally new.'

43 Finson, 'Performing practice', p. 474.

44 See Bryant, 'Brahms' Clarinet Quintet – what the critics said'; 'The clarinet on record', p. 206.

45 The first movement is cut from bars 25 to 147; the second begins at the *Più lento* (bar 52), and is cut from bars 58 to 63, and from 88 to 127.

46 This and subsequent reviews are cited from Bryant, 'Brahms' Clarinet Quintet'.

47 See the notes by Charles Haynes to the 1991 reissue of Draper's recording on Pearl (Gemm CD 9903). Thurston's second recording (1941) with the Griller Quartet (Decca AR5738/45) was never issued.

48 Amodio was active in Germany in the 1930s and 1940s, recording with German musicians (for Siemens, Polydor and Electrola) the Mozart Concerto and Quintet, the Beethoven Trio and the Brahms F minor Sonata.

49 Philip, *Early Recordings*, pp. 130–1.

50 Eldering had turned the pages when Brahms and Joachim gave the first performance of the D minor Violin Sonata Op. 108 and had played all three sonatas with the composer. Busch was also a composition pupil of Steinbach and showed Brahms's influence in his own music.

7 The legacy of Brahms's clarinet music

1 Kroll's *Die Klarinette* was published only in 1965 (Eng. trans. 1968), some twenty years after the author's death in action.

2 Amongst other composers for clarinet trio were Robert Kahn (first performed in 1905 by Mühlfeld), Johannes Amberg (1912) and Karl Frühling (1925). Max Bruch preferred an ensemble with viola for his *Acht Stücke* Op. 83 of 1910. Sonatas by G. Bumcke (1905) and by Hans Pogge (1912) were reviewed by Tuthill (*Cobbett's Cyclopaedic Survey of Chamber Music*, I, p. 280) as respectively 'Not vitally interesting' and 'well made

German music, but says nothing much.' He wrote of Egon Kornauth's Sonata (1922), 'a striving after something which does not seem to come off'.

3 I am grateful to Michael Bryant for a list of Mühlfeld's repertory, compiled from the clarinettist's diary in the possession of the Mühlfeld family. It comprises duos with piano, chamber music in various combinations and works with orchestra.

4 Thomas Dunhill, *Chamber Music*, p. 247.

5 Weston, *More Clarinet Virtuosi*, p. 180, notes that Mühlfeld performed Krehl's Quintet at Karlsruhe on 30 October 1901.

6 A trio dedicated to Kürmeyer is now lost. See Pamela Weston, 'Players and composers', p. 98.

7 Quoted from Kroll, *The Clarinet*, pp. 82–3.

8 Kroll, *ibid.*, p. 83.

9 See *Clarinet & Saxophone* 9/1 (1984), p. 34.

10 Christopher Palmer's note to Thea King's recording (Hyperion CDA 66479) cites the *Neue Freie Presse Wien*, which heard in this quintet 'the scents and colours of soft spring blossoms set to music'.

11 R. Heuberger, ed. K. Hofmann, *Erinnerungen an Johannes Brahms*, p. 48. As Pascall notes in his article 'Robert Fuchs', p. 115, this interest in Fuchs also tells us something about Brahms.

12 Oscar Street,'The clarinet and its music', p. 108. Silvertrust, 'Beyond Brahms and Mozart', p. 5, remarks that if Dvořák had written a clarinet quintet it might not have been far different from this. However, Stephen Banfield's appraisal of Coleridge-Taylor's style in *The New Grove* can justifiably be applied to certain parts of the Quintet: 'Too often he relies on wholesale repetition of a motif which is not strong or flexible enough to bear it.'

13 John Ireland's Sextet of 1898, which adds a horn to the ensemble, owes its inspiration to Mühlfeld's performance of the Brahms Quintet. His near contemporary Richard Walthew (1872–1951) wrote an unpublished clarinet quintet *c.* 1918.

14 Scored for bass clarinet and string quartet.

15 Rendall, *The Clarinet*, p. 179.

16 Somervell, like Brahms, writes an impassioned first movement in compound duple time; he follows this with a gentle Intermezzo, a slow movement consisiting of variations, and a sparkling finale. Michael Hurd's stylistic appraisal in *The New Grove* can with justification be applied to the Quintet: 'his music is grounded in the German classics, lying somewhere between Mendelssohn and Brahms in an area which was perhaps

more adequately explored by Parry'. The Quintet was finally published by Emerson in 1984.

17 Andrew Keener in a note to Janet Hilton's recording of 1983 (Chandos 86360).

18 For a wide-ranging survey, see Roger Heaton, 'The contemporary clarinet', in *The Cambridge Companion to the Clarinet*', pp. 163–83.

Appendices

1 The right-hand ring mechanism which improved $b/f\sharp''$ (replacing Müller's key) had been developed by Adolphe Sax, allowing R1–3 effectively to control four toneholes.

Select bibliography

Altenburg, W., *Die Klarinette* (Heilbronn, 1904)

Baermann, C., *Vollständige Clarinetten-Schule* (Offenbach, 1864–75)

Baines, A., *Woodwind Instruments and their History* (London, 1957; 3rd edn, 1967)

Birsak, K., *Die Klarinette: Eine Kulturgeschichte* (Buchloe, 1992; trans. G. Schamberger, 1994)

Brixel, E., *Klarinetten-Bibliographie* (Wilhelmshaven, 1978)

Brown, C., 'Bowing styles, vibrato and portamento in nineteenth-century violin-playing', *Journal of the Royal Musical Association* 113/1 (1988), pp. 97–128

Bryant, M., 'Brahms' Clarinet Quintet – what the critics said', *Clarinet & Saxophone* 9/3 (1984), pp. 6–7, and 9/4 (1984), pp. 14–17

'The clarinet on record', in *The Cambridge Companion to the Clarinet*, ed. Colin Lawson (Cambridge, 1995), pp. 199–212

Brymer, J., *Clarinet* (London, 1976)

Clark, D., 'Reflections on Mühlfeld', *Clarinet & Saxophone* 14/1 (1989), p. 14

Cobbett, W. W., *Cobbett's Cyclopaedic Survey of Chamber Music* (Oxford, 1929/R1963)

Colles, H. C., *The Chamber Music of Brahms* (Oxford, 1933)

Derenburg, C., 'My recollections of Brahms', *Musical Times* 67 (1926), pp. 598–600

Dunhill, T. F., *Chamber Music* (London, 1913)

Dyson, G., 'Brahms's Clarinet Quintet Op. 115', *Musical Times* 76 (1935), pp. 315–19

Evans, E., *Handbook to the Chamber and Orchestral Music of Johannes Brahms* (London, 1933–5)

Fay, J. S., 'The Clarinet and its Use as a Solo Instrument in the Chamber Music of Johannes Brahms', DMA, Peabody Conservatory of Music, Baltimore (1991)

Finson, J. W., 'Performing practice in the late nineteenth century, with special reference to the music of Brahms', *The Musical Quarterly* 70/4 (1984), pp. 457–75

Flesch, C., *The Art of Violin Playing*, 2 vols. (New York, 1924; 1930)

Forsyth, C., *Orchestration* (London, 1914, 2nd edn, 1935)

Foster, P., 'Brahms, Schenker and the Rules of Composition: Compositional and theoretical problems in the clarinet works', Ph.D. diss., University of Reading (1994)

Frisch, W., *Brahms and the Principle of Developing Variation* (Berkeley and Los Angeles, 1984)

Garlick, N. B., 'Charles Villiers Stanford & his five works for clarinet', *The Clarinet* 21/4 (1994), pp. 28–32

Geiringer, K., *Brahms: his Life and Work*, trans. H. B. Weiner and B. Miall (London, 1948/R1982)

Graham, J. E., 'An Analysis of Brahms's Quintet in B minor, Op. 115, for Clarinet and Strings', M.A. diss., North Texas State University (1968)

Häfner, R., *Johannes Brahms, Klarinettenquintett* in *Meisterwerke der Musik* 14 (Munich, 1978)

Heuberger, R., *Johannes Brahms, I. Trio ... op. 114, II. Quintett ... op. 115 (Der Musikführer no. 45)* (Frankfurt am Main, 1895)

Erinnerungen an Johannes Brahms, ed. K. Hofmann (Tutzing, 1971)

Jenner, G., *Johannes Brahms als Mensch, Lehrer und Künstler: Studien und Erlebnisse* (Marburg, 1905)

Joachim, J., and Moser, A., *Violinschule* (Berlin, 1902–5)

Kell, R., 'The clarinet music of Johannes Brahms', *Woodwind World* 4/3 (1960), p. 5

Keys, I., *Brahms Chamber Music* (Seattle, 1974)

Kroll, O., *Die Klarinette* (Kassel, 1965; trans. H. Morris, ed. A. Baines, London, 1968)

Kross, S., 'The establishment of a Brahms repertoire 1890–1902', in *Brahms 2: Biographical, Documentary and Analytical Studies*, ed. M. Musgrave (Cambridge, 1987), pp. 21–38

Langwill, L. G., *An Index of Musical Woodwind Makers* (Edinburgh, 1960; rev. enlarged 6th edn, 1980), rev. W. Waterhouse as *The New Langwill Index* (London, 1993)

Lawson, C., *Mozart Clarinet Concerto* (Cambridge, 1996)

Lawson, C. (ed.), *The Cambridge Companion to the Clarinet* (Cambridge, 1995)

Litzmann, B. (ed.), *Letters of Clara Schumann and Johannes Brahms 1853–1896* (London, 1927)

Maas, G. L., 'Problems of Form in the Clarinet Quintet of Brahms', M.A. diss., University of Wisconsin (1967)

MacDonald, M., *Brahms* (London, 1990)

Mason, D. G., *The Chamber Music of Brahms* (New York, 1933)

May, F., *The Life of Johannes Brahms* (London, 1905; 2nd edn, 1948)

Mayr, A., *Erinnerungen an Robert Fuchs* (Graz, 1934)

McCorkle, M. L., *Brahms Werkverzeichnis* (Munich, 1984)

Moser, A., *Joseph Joachim*, trans. Lilla Durham (London, 1901)

Mühlfeld, C., *Die herzogliche Hofkapelle in Meiningen* (Meiningen, 1910)

Musgrave, M., *The Music of Brahms* (London, 1985)

Musgrave, M. and Pascall, R., 'The string quartets op. 51 no. 1 in C minor and no. 2 in A minor', in *Brahms 2: Biographical, Documentary and Analytical Studies*, ed. Musgrave (Cambridge, 1987), pp. 137–43

Notley, M., 'Brahms as liberal: genre, style and politics in nineteenth-century Vienna', *19th-Century Music* 17/2 (1993), pp. 107–23

Opperman, K., *Repertory of the Clarinet* (New York, 1960)

Pascall, R. J., 'Formal Principles in the Music of Brahms', D.Phil. diss., University of Oxford (1973)

'Robert Fuchs, 1847–1927', *Musical Times* 118 (1977), pp. 115–17

'Ruminations on Brahms's chamber music', *Musical Times* 116 (1975), pp. 697–9

'Some special uses of sonata form by Brahms', *Soundings* 4 (1974), pp. 58–63

Philip, R., *Early Recordings and Musical Style* (Cambridge, 1992)

Portnoy, B., 'Brahms' Prima Donna', *Woodwind World* 4 (15 February 1963), pp. 12–13

Rendall, F. G., *The Clarinet* (London, 1954; rev. 3rd edn by P. Bate, 1971)

'The clarinet in England', *Proceedings of the Musical Association* 68 (1942), pp. 55–86

Schauffler, R. H., *The Unknown Brahms: his Life, Character and Works, Based on New Material* (New York, 1933)

Schoenberg, A., *Fundamentals of Musical Composition*, ed. G. Strang and L. Stein (London, 1967)

Style and Idea: Selected Writings of Arnold Schoenberg, ed. L. Stein (London, 1975)

Schumann, F., 'Brahms and Clara Schumann', trans. J. Mayer, *The Musical Quarterly* 16 (1933), p. 515

Seggelke, J., 'Die Baermann-Ottensteiner-Klarinette im musikgeschichtlichen Kontext', *Rohrblatt* 11/1 (1996), pp. 2–5

Shackleton, N., and Puddy, K., 'Mühlfeld's clarinets', *Clarinet & Saxophone* 14/1 (1989), pp. 26–7

Shaw, G. B., *Music in London, 1890–4* (London, 1931/*R*1973)

Silvertrust, R. H. R., 'Beyond Brahms and Mozart – other clarinet quintets', *Journal of the Cobbett Association* 6/2 (1995), pp. 5–6

Stahmer, K., 'Korrekturen am Brahmsbild: Eine Studie zur musikalischen Fehlinterpretation', *Die Musikforschung* 25/2 (1972), pp. 152–67

Stowell, R. (ed.), *The Cambridge Companion to the Violin* (Cambridge, 1992)

Street, O. W., 'The clarinet and its music', *Proceedings of the Musical Association* 42 (1916), pp. 89–115

Tovey, D. F., 'Brahms', in *Cobbett's Cyclopaedic Survey of Chamber Music* (Oxford, 1929/*R*1963), I, pp.158–85

'Brahms chamber music', in *Essays and Lectures on Music* (Oxford, 1949), pp. 220–70

Tuthill, B. C., 'The clarinet in chamber music', in *Cobbett's Cyclopaedic Survey of Chamber Music* (Oxford, 1929/*R*1963), I, pp. 279–82

Weston, P., *Clarinet Virtuosi of the Past* (London, 1971)

'Meine Primadonna – Brahms' Clarinettist', *Clarinet & Saxophone* 13/3 (1988), pp. 27–30

More Clarinet Virtuosi of the Past (London, 1977)

'Players and composers', in *The Cambridge Companion to the Clarinet*, ed. Colin Lawson (Cambridge, 1995), 92–106

Wilke, R., *Brahms, Reger, Schoenberg Streichquartette: Motivisch-thematische Prozesse und formale Gestalt* (Hamburg, 1980)

Index